AF714937

"A bold roadmap for navigating the new world of work."

– **Dr. J. Alexander Martin,** Co-founder, FUBU

"For over twenty-plus years, I have lived by the edicts of Dr. Chamberlain of Harvard University who suggested there are three reasons to change: 1) You are behind, 2) You can see others catching up and 3) You see the landscape changing. Mike Johns has written a timely and necessary book. Death of a Job is more than insight—it's a mission-critical call to prepare our communities, our workforce, and our nation for a future we can't afford to ignore."

– Brigadier General (Ret.) **Arnold Gordon-Bray**

"A wake-up call!"

– **Sophia the Robot**

"A masterclass in what's next ..."

– **Vin Rock**, Founding Member - Naughty By Nature

DEATH OF A JOB

The Future of Work in the Age of AI

BY MIKE JOHNS

Copyright © 2025 by Mike Johns. All rights reserved.

No part of this publication may be reproduced, distributed or transmitted in any form or by any means, including photocopying, recording or other electronic methods, without the prior written permission of the publisher, except in cases of brief quotations.

ISBN: 979-8-9996257-3-1

DEDICATION

To my son, who has been my greatest inspiration and guiding light, this book is dedicated to you above all.

DEATH OF A JOB

The Future of Work in the Age of AI

BY MIKE JOHNS

"What do we do about massive unemployment? This is going to be a massive social challenge. There will be fewer jobs that a robot cannot do better. I think ultimately, we have to have some sort of universal basic income. I don't think we are going to have a choice. The harder challenge, the much harder challenge is how do people have meaning? A lot of people derive their meaning from employment. If you're not needed, if there is not a need for your labor, do you have meaning? Do you feel useless?"

– **Elon Musk** (World Government Summit, 2017)

"We, as the producers of this technology, have a duty and an obligation to be honest about what's coming", he said. "I don't think this is on people's radar."

– **Dario Amodei,** CEO, Anthropic

CONTENTS

THE ROLE OF AI IN THE DEVELOPMENT OF THIS MANUSCRIPT

The integration of artificial intelligence into our daily workflows has become the new normal— similar to how spell check became the norm nearly two decades ago. As someone who strongly advocates for transparency in the use of AI, I believe it's important to communicate how AI contributed to the development of this manuscript.

Specifically, AI was utilized to help organize my raw notes, structure my transcribed ideas, support research and data gathering, recommend relevant sources, and assist with the compilation of citations and references.

This book not only discusses the future of human-AI collaboration—it also reflects it. References for each chapter are included at the end of the book.

PREFACE

DEATH OF A JOB, LABOR AND WORK AS WE KNOW IT

"Stay hungry, Stay Foolish."
– Steve Jobs

Welcome to *Death of a Job*, a journey into the rapidly evolving world of work, where the old rules are fading, and new possibilities are emerging. As the traditional concept of "jobs" centered around a nine-to-five grind gives way to a landscape defined by flexibility, hybrid work, and continuous learning, we find ourselves at a pivotal moment in history. This book invites you to embrace the adventure of the unknown, to explore the vast potential that lies beyond the confines of employment.

Death of a Job is not about lamenting the loss of a steady paycheck or a neat cubicle. Instead, it's about how technology is liberating work from the shackles of jobs, recognizing that work exists beyond contractual agreements – in entrepreneurship, freelancing, volunteering, and the pursuit of personal passions. It's about understanding that humans are inherently wired for work, for purpose, and for the joy of making a difference in the world.

Here, we'll delve into the importance of entrepreneurship and innovation, recognizing that with access to the right tools and platforms, anyone can create their own opportunities and forge their own destiny. We will also confront head-on the disruptive nature of AI and its impact on the job market, offering insights and customized roadmaps to help you unlearn, relearn, and reskill for the future.

Death of a Job is your guide to navigating this new terrain, to finding fulfillment in a world where work is no longer defined by a job title, but by the passion, drive, and sense of purpose that flow through your veins. So, buckle up, embrace the adventure, and prepare to unlock your superpower – your ability to make a dent in the universe. The future of work is here, and it's not about jobs, it's about you.

CHAPTER 1

AMERICA'S NEW BEGINNING

"Once a new technology rolls over you, if you're not part of the steamroller, you're part of the road."
– **Stewart Brand,** Tech Visionary and Co-Chair, the *Long Now Foundation*

The next five years is more important than the last fifty, with the Trump administration now in charge, Peter Thiel's libertarian ideology and the rapid evolution of artificial intelligence (AI) is reshaping the future of work in America. Death of a Job explores how these forces are transforming labor markets, redefining gender dynamics, and setting the tone for workforce policies over the next five years.

The Libertarian Foundation: Thiel's Vision for Governance and Technology

Peter Thiel's 2009 essay, *"The Education of a Libertarian,"* laid the groundwork for a techno-libertarian approach to governance. Thiel argued that democracy often impedes innovation and freedom, advocating for minimal government intervention and elite-driven technological advancement. His vision emphasized leveraging technology to bypass traditional political systems, creating spaces for experimentation free from democratic oversight.

This ideology profoundly influenced Project 2025, which seeks to dismantle federal agencies, reduce public assistance programs, and deregulate industries. AI plays a central role in this framework, enabling automation that reduces reliance on human labor while concentrating power in private-sector entities. Thiel's belief in "creative destruction" aligns with the administration's push to replace outdated systems with AI-driven efficiencies.

The Trump Administration's AI Agenda

Although not associated with Project 2025, President Trump has made AI a cornerstone of his policy agenda. His administration has prioritized American leadership in AI by removing regulatory barriers established under previous administrations. A executive order revoked Biden-era policies that imposed government oversight on AI development, clearing the path for private-sector innovation.

Key elements of Trump's AI agenda include:

- **Enhancing National Security:** AI is being leveraged to counter foreign interference and bolster cybersecurity.
- **Economic Competitiveness:** By doubling research investments and establishing national AI research institutes, the administration aims to secure America's dominance in global AI innovation.
- **Workforce Transformation:** Federal agencies are adopting AI to streamline operations and reduce costs, setting a precedent for broader workplace automation.

These initiatives reflect the libertarian ideals espoused by Thiel by prioritizing technological progress over democratic accountability.

AI and Job Displacement: A Double-Edged Sword

AI is projected to disrupt employment patterns significantly over the next five years. According to the World Economic Forum's *Future of Jobs Report 2025*, advances in AI will create 19 million jobs while displacing 9 million others. Automation is expected to affect men and women differently:

Impact on Men

- Male-dominated industries like manufacturing and logistics face high risks of job displacement due to automation.
- Truck driving and factory assembly roles are particularly vulnerable as autonomous systems become more prevalent.

Impact on Women

- Women are disproportionately affected by automation in clerical and administrative roles. For example, 85% of bank tellers—predominantly women—are at high risk of replacement.
- Gender biases embedded in AI algorithms could exacerbate existing inequalities in hiring and promotion processes unless addressed proactively.

Black, Indigenous and People of Color (BIPOC) workers are likely to face disproportionate challenges due to structural inequalities embedded in the labor market.

Impact on BIPOC Communities

- **Concentration in Vulnerable Roles:** BIPOC workers are overrepresented in industries most susceptible to automation, such as manufacturing, logistics, and administrative support. These roles are among the first targeted for replacement by autonomous systems.
- **Algorithmic Bias:** Without regulatory oversight, AI systems used in hiring and promotion decisions can perpetuate discriminatory biases. Studies have shown

that automated tools often rank candidates from marginalized backgrounds lower than their equally qualified counterparts.

- **Economic Hardship:** Regions with high concentrations of BIPOC workers—particularly rural and urban areas reliant on manufacturing—may experience severe economic disruption as automation replaces traditional jobs.

The Role of Deregulation

In early 2025, Trump's executive orders removed critical protections designed to mitigate these impacts. For example:

- The Equal Employment Opportunity Commission (EEOC) has scaled back guidance on using AI responsibly in hiring processes under Title VII anti-discrimination laws.
- Federal contractors are no longer required to comply with best practices for ensuring equity in AI-driven employment decisions.

This deregulation leaves businesses free to adopt AI systems without addressing potential harms, placing the burden on workers—particularly those from marginalized communities—to navigate an increasingly opaque job market.

Implications for Equity Over the Next Five Years

The Trump administration's approach to AI sets a tone for the next five years that **prioritizes innovation over inclusivity.** While technological advancements promise efficiency gains and economic growth, they also risk deepening systemic inequalities. For BIPOC communities, this means navigating an increasingly automated workforce with fewer protections against bias and displacement.

Critical Questions Moving Forward

1. Will businesses integrate ethical safeguards into their AI systems without being required by federal mandates?
2. What role should state governments play in protecting marginalized workers from **algorithmic discrimination?**
3. How can public-private partnerships ensure equitable access to reskilling programs?

The answers to these questions will determine whether AI serves as a tool for empowerment or a mechanism of exclusion for workers and BIPOC.

Metric	Current Impact on BIPOC Workers	Projected Impact by 2030
Job Displacement	High in manufacturing/ logistics	Increased vulnerability
Algorithmic Bias	Significant	Worsening without oversight
Reskilling Participation	Low due to access barriers	Potential growth with targeted programs

(Data source: Workforce Bulletin & World Economic Forum)

These insights underscore the urgent need for equity-focused policies as America navigates its workforce transformation by 2030.

Implications for Gender Equality

AI has the potential to narrow or widen gender gaps in the workforce. On one hand, automation could eliminate biases in recruiting and evaluation processes. On the other hand, women remain more vulnerable to job displacement due to their concentration in roles susceptible to automation.

Strategies for Mitigation

- **Reskilling Programs:** Companies must invest in training initiatives to prepare women for high-growth technological roles.
- **Algorithmic Transparency:** Ensuring that AI systems are free from gender biases is critical for equitable outcomes.
- **Leadership Opportunities:** Promoting women into senior positions can insulate them from automation risks while fostering diversity.

Setting the Tone for the Next Five Years

AI signals a radical transformation in America's workforce policies:

1. **Dismantling Traditional Systems:** Federal agencies are being streamlined through automation, reducing public-sector employment.
2. **Private-Sector Dominance:** The concentration of power among tech elites aligns with **Thiel's vision of governance driven by innovation rather than democracy.**
3. **Workforce Disruption:** Millions of jobs will be displaced or transformed by AI technologies.
4. **Gender Dynamics:** Women face unique challenges but also opportunities as workplaces adapt to automation.

As America transitions into this new era, balancing technological progress with social equity will be essential. The choices made today will shape not only the future of work but also the broader societal implications of AI-driven governance.

Metric	Current (2025)	Projected (2030)
Jobs Created by AI	19 million	~69 million
Jobs Displaced by Automation	9 million	~83 million
Human-Machine Task Division	Humans: 47%	Humans: ~33%
Gender-Based Job Risk (Women)	~11%	Higher Risk

(Data source: World Economic Forum Future of Jobs Report 2025)

These statistics highlight both the challenges and opportunities posed by AI as America navigates its workforce transformation.

Trump's AI Vision: Innovation Without a Net?

President Trump's bold approach to AI policy marks a pivotal moment in shaping the future of work. While his agenda accelerates innovation and economic growth, it also places significant responsibility on businesses to address ethical challenges independently. As AI continues to disrupt industries, leaders must proactively adapt workforce strategies to harness its potential while mitigating risks. The success of this transformation will depend on balancing technological advancements with human ingenuity—a challenge that defines the future of work in America.

CHAPTER 2

TRUMP AND THE END OF CAPITALISM?

"It's easier to imagine the end of the world than the end of capitalism."
– **Fredric Jameson** and **Slavoj Žižek**

In 2024, the Biden administration took significant steps to address the risks of artificial intelligence (AI), introducing measures to protect against bias and discrimination while fostering responsible development. These efforts included the landmark *Executive Order on Safe, Secure, and Trustworthy Development and Use of Artificial Intelligence*, signed in October 2023, which emphasized oversight, equity, and accountability across AI systems. The order directed federal agencies to combat algorithmic discrimination, ensure transparency in AI-generated content, and safeguard civil rights in areas such as housing, healthcare, and government benefits. Major companies like Google also pledged to uphold principles of responsible AI development, committing to safety-first systems and ethical standards.

However, under President Donald Trump's administration, this trajectory has shifted dramatically. On his first day in office in January 2025, Trump rescinded Biden's executive order through his own directive titled *Removing Barriers to American Leadership in Artificial Intelligence*. This new policy prioritizes deregulation and innovation over oversight and risk mitigation. It explicitly criticizes "engineered social agendas" in AI systems and removes safeguards designed to address bias, disinformation, and equity concerns. The Trump administration's approach frames AI development as a matter of national competitiveness and economic strength while reducing federal oversight.

Simultaneously, major corporations like Google have rolled back their own responsible AI principles. Once committed to limiting the use of AI for military applications or surveillance systems that undermine human rights, Google has replaced these guidelines with vague commitments to "create AI that protects people" while supporting national security interests. This rollback coincides with Trump's deregulatory stance on AI governance which raises concerns about the potential misuse of AI technologies in sensitive areas such as military weapons and surveillance.

The implications of these shifts are profound. Without safeguards or accountability measures, AI systems risk exacerbating societal harms such as algorithmic bias, discrimination, and disinformation. Vulnerable populations, including BIPOC communities—face heightened risks as protections against automated inequities are dismantled. Additionally, the rollback of responsible AI principles by corporations like Google signals a troubling trend where profit motives may override ethical considerations.

The contrast between Biden's holistic approach to AI regulation and Trump's deregulatory framework underscores the stakes for society at large. While Biden sought to balance innovation with equity and safety through collaboration between government, industry, and civil society, Trump's policies prioritize rapid development at the expense of oversight. As AI continues to reshape critical sectors such as healthcare, housing, and law enforcement, the absence of robust safeguards could lead to significant societal consequences.

In this new era of AI governance under Trump, the need for transparency, accountability, and ethical standards has never been more urgent. Without these measures in place, the transformative potential of AI may be overshadowed by its capacity to deepen inequalities and erode trust in technology.

AI in Trump's Capitalist Vision

Under Trump's leadership, AI is positioned as a tool for enhancing American economic dominance and competitiveness. The administration's policies aim to:

1. Remove regulatory barriers to AI innovation
2. Encourage private sector leadership in AI development
3. Prioritize U.S. technological supremacy over regulatory caution

This approach aligns with a laissez-faire capitalist model, where government intervention is minimized to allow market forces to drive advancement in AI.

The Fate of Economic Models

The rapid advancement of AI under this deregulated approach is likely to accelerate the obsolescence of current economic models:

1. **Labor Market Disruption**: As AI capabilities expand, traditional concepts of employment and labor **value** are being fundamentally challenged.
2. **Productivity Paradox**: While AI promises unprecedented productivity gains, it may also lead to widespread job displacement, potentially disrupting conventional economic growth models. Globally, AI could replace nearly 800 million jobs by 2030.
3. **Income Distribution**: The concentration of AI benefits in the hands of a few may exacerbate income

inequality, challenging existing **models of wealth distribution.**

4. **Value of Money**: As AI reshapes economic structures, the traditional concept of money and its value may need to be reevaluated. Digital currencies and AI-driven financial systems could potentially alter the very nature of monetary transactions and value storage.

The Socioeconomic Contract in Flux

The current socioeconomic contract, based on the exchange of labor for wages within a capitalist framework, is becoming increasingly untenable:

1. **Job Displacement**: The AI EO's focus on removing barriers to AI development may accelerate job losses across various sectors, including government.
2. **Social Safety Nets**: Traditional unemployment and welfare systems may prove inadequate in an AI-dominated economy, requiring new models of social support.
3. **Education and Skill Development**: The rapid pace of AI advancement is outstripping current educational systems' ability to prepare workers for the future job market.
4. **Power Dynamics**: The concentration of AI capabilities in the hands of a few corporations and government entities may lead to unprecedented power imbalances in society.

Government Transformation: The DOGE Case Study

The Department of Government Efficiency (DOGE), under the leadership of Elon Musk, is a stark example of how AI is being used to reshape the federal workforce and is a peek into the future of work in government agencies under an AI-driven paradigm:

1. **AI-Driven Job Displacement**: Musk's implementation of AI systems at DOGE led to significant job cuts, with many federal workers being replaced by AI technologies.
2. **Workplace Culture Shift**: Musk's management style at DOGE, characterized by ultimatums and demands for increased productivity, led to a tense work environment.
3. **Legal and Ethical Challenges**: The rapid integration of AI at DOGE raised questions about the legality and ethics of replacing federal workers with AI systems.

The Need for a Plan fast!

As of the writing of this manuscript, there does not appear to be a comprehensive plan in place to address the massive socioeconomic disruptions that AI is poised to create. The stark contrast between the Biden and Trump administrations' approaches to AI governance sets the stage for a transformative period in government work and the broader economy.

The integration of AI into federal agencies and private sectors has the potential to radically reshape the workforce, raising critical questions about the future role of human workers. The ongoing debate between regulation and innovation in AI policy will play a crucial role in determining how this transformation unfolds, with far-reaching consequences for both government employees and the services they provide to the public.

To address these challenges, I cannot help but emphasize that a multifaceted approach involving government, industry, and civil society will be necessary to:

1. Develop new economic models that account for AI's impact on labor and value creation
2. Create adaptive education and retraining "Be Skilled" programs
3. Design new social safety nets for the AI era

4. Establish ethical guidelines for AI development and deployment

Without such a plan, the rapid advancement of AI under the current deregulatory approach risks exacerbating social inequalities and economic instabilities, potentially leading to widespread societal disruption.

The Future of Jobs in an AI-Driven Economy

The implications of President Donald Trump's Executive Order 14179 extends significantly into labor markets. By 2030, AI technologies are projected to have dramatically reshaped employment landscapes worldwide, while simultaneously creating new opportunities and displacing traditional roles. According to projections from the World Economic Forum (WEF), AI will generate approximately 170 million new jobs globally while displacing around 92 million existing role-resulting in a net gain of roughly 78 million jobs.

Projected job creation and displacement by 2030

Category	Millions
Jobs Created	170
Jobs Displaced	92
Net Job Gain	78

(Data source: World Economic Forum)

These figures underscore both AI's transformative potential and the urgency for workers and organizations to swiftly adapt.

Emerging Roles and Essential Skills

The rapid increase in AI-related job postings highlights this shift. In October 2024 alone, over 16,000 AI-focused positions were advertised, reflecting strong demand for specialized roles such as Generative AI Engineers and Computer Vision Engineers. Beyond technical competencies—including Python programming, TensorFlow, PyTorch, and natural language processing—uniquely human skills like critical thinking, creativity, adaptability, and collaboration will become increasingly valuable. Workers will increasingly occupy augmented roles where strategic decision-making is emphasized while repetitive tasks are delegated to AI systems.

Industry Transformations Driven by AI

The Trump administration's policy aims to accelerate transformative changes across multiple sectors. By 2030, key industries are expected to experience significant shifts:

Healthcare:

- Enhanced diagnostics through advanced AI-powered tools.
- Robotic surgery assistants improving surgical precision.
- Healthcare professionals collaborating closely with AI systems in patient management.

Customer Service:

- Routine inquiries managed by sophisticated chatbots.
- Human representatives focusing on complex issues requiring empathy and nuanced judgment.

Marketing:

- AI-driven tools optimizing campaigns and personalizing customer interactions.
- Marketers integrating technical expertise with creative strategies.

Finance:

- Automated trading systems and fraud detection algorithms dominating routine operations.

- Finance professionals overseeing ethical practices and strategic decision-making alongside these automated systems.

Opportunities vs. Risks: The Importance of Guardrails

While prioritizing rapid innovation by removing perceived barriers, this approach raises important concerns about potential risks associated with insufficiently regulated or improperly implemented AI systems:

- **Job Displacement Without Adequate Support:** Workers in routine roles risk struggling without comprehensive retraining initiatives.
- **Potential for Discrimination:** Automated hiring platforms or gamified assessments could inadvertently perpetuate biases if not carefully designed.
- **Risks in Government Applications:** Poorly deployed automated systems could result in costly errors or unfair outcomes in critical areas such as social benefits distribution or fraud detection.

These risks highlight the necessity of balancing accelerated innovation with ethical considerations. Common-sense safeguards—including transparency requirements, bias audits, and robust worker protections—are essential to ensuring that technological progress benefits all segments of society.

The Fate of Work in the Age of AI

AI has the potential to dismantle systemic barriers, such as eliminating racist restrictions in housing covenants and improving access to government benefits. However, it also carries the risk of perpetuating inequities, such as denying individuals health care or mortgages based on biased algorithms tied to race. Recognizing this dual-edged nature of AI, Democratic Assemblymember Rebecca Bauer-Kahan of

San Ramon, CA introduced legislation in March of 2025—for the third consecutive year—aimed at protecting people from automated discrimination. Her bill seeks to ensure that AI systems making life-altering decisions are held accountable and operate fairly, safeguarding individuals from the unintended harms of unchecked technology.

Key factoids:

1. **Deregulation at the Federal Level**
   President Trump has prioritized loosening AI regulations by repealing Biden-era executive orders that imposed voluntary guardrails on AI development. This approach accelerates innovation but raises concerns about ethical oversight and worker protections. Without safeguards, AI systems risk exacerbating existing inequalities while prioritizing efficiency over fairness.
2. **AI as a Tool for Enforcement**
   Federal agencies like Homeland Security are increasingly deploying AI tools for tasks such as immigration enforcement and surveillance. Technologies like RAVE (Real-Time Analytical Video Environment) expand the scope of monitoring but disproportionately affect vulnerable populations, including undocumented immigrants. This raises ethical concerns about how AI is used in governance and law enforcement.
3. **Job Displacement Risks**
   Automation powered by AI is expected to replace millions of jobs across industries like manufacturing, logistics, and clerical work. Workers in these sectors face significant challenges transitioning to new roles without targeted reskilling programs. The absence of federal initiatives to support displaced workers leaves many at risk of long-term unemployment or economic instability.

4. **Algorithmic Bias Concerns**
   The removal of fairness and safety language from federal AI guidelines risks perpetuating systemic biases in hiring, promotions, and workplace monitoring systems. BIPOC workers and other marginalized groups are particularly vulnerable to discriminatory practices embedded in algorithmic decision-making.
5. **Rise of Algorithmic Management**
   AI-driven tools are increasingly being used to monitor employee performance and enforce workplace policies. While these systems improve efficiency for employers, they often reduce worker autonomy, raise privacy concerns, and create environments where employees feel surveilled rather than empowered.
6. **California's Leadership in AI Regulation**
   In contrast to federal deregulation, California has passed numerous AI-related laws addressing issues like digital identity theft, election misinformation, and discriminatory practices. These efforts position California as a model for rights-respecting AI governance, emphasizing transparency and accountability in technology deployment.
7. **Tensions Between Federal and State Policies**
   Trump's deregulatory approach clashes with California's stricter AI laws, creating a growing divide between federal priorities and state-level safeguards. This tension could lead to legal battles over preemption of state regulations, with implications for how AI is governed nationwide.
8. **Economic Inequality Amplified by Automation**
   Without proactive measures to address job displacement, wealth generated by AI is likely to remain concentrated among tech elites while low-income workers face growing economic insecurity. Automation risks deepening economic divides unless policies are

implemented to ensure equitable distribution of benefits.

9. **Opportunities for Reskilling**
   Despite its challenges, AI presents opportunities for workforce transformation if investments are made in reskilling programs that prepare workers for high-demand fields like cybersecurity, renewable energy, and healthcare. These initiatives could help displaced workers transition into new roles while fostering economic growth.
10. **The Need for Transparency**
   Both federal and state governments must prioritize transparency in how AI systems are developed and deployed to ensure accountability and prevent misuse across industries. Clear guidelines are essential to maintaining public trust while mitigating risks associated with automation.

Why The "How" Matters

The integration of AI into the workforce is not just a technological shift—it is a societal transformation that will define the future of work for generations to come. The decisions made today will determine whether AI serves as a tool for empowerment or exacerbates existing inequalities:

- **For Workers:** Millions face uncertainty as automation replaces traditional roles without clear pathways for reskilling or redeployment.
- **For Vulnerable Populations:** Marginalized groups—including BIPOC workers—are disproportionately impacted by algorithmic bias and job displacement.
- **For States vs Federal Government:** The divide between California's proactive regulations and Trump's deregulatory stance highlights conflicting visions for how technology should be governed.

- **For Economic Equity:** Without safeguards, wealth generated by AI will concentrate among tech elites while leaving low-income workers behind.
- **For Society at Large:** Transparency and accountability are critical to ensuring that AI systems align with ethical standards while fostering innovation responsibly.

Navigating the Challenges Ahead

The rapid adoption of AI technologies presents both opportunities and risks that require thoughtful management:

1. **Reskilling Programs:** Investments in retraining initiatives can prepare displaced workers for high-demand fields like cybersecurity or healthcare while equipping them with skills to thrive alongside AI tools.
2. **Ethical Oversight:** Businesses must prioritize audits of their AI systems to mitigate algorithmic bias and ensure fair treatment across all demographics.
3. **Collaboration Across Sectors:** Governments, educational institutions, and private companies must work together to create pathways that support workers through this transition.
4. **State-Level Leadership:** States like California can serve as models for rights-respecting governance by implementing laws that balance innovation with equity.
5. **Transparency Mandates:** Clear guidelines on how data is collected, analyzed, and utilized by AI systems will be essential in building public trust.

As America navigates the AI workforce , balancing innovation with equity will be crucial to creating a future where technology serves all members of society—not just a privileged few. By addressing these challenges head-on through thoughtful policies and collaboration between federal and state governments, the nation can harness the transformative power of AI while safeguarding its workforce against unintended consequences.

The Government's Awareness of AI's Impact on Work

The U.S. government is well aware of AI's profound implications for employment and economic structures. Policymakers understand that artificial intelligence will fundamentally reshape labor markets by automating routine tasks while simultaneously creating new roles requiring distinctly human capabilities such as creativity and strategic insight.

As discussed by experts such as former special advisor for artificial intelligence in the Biden White House, Ben Buchanan, government officials recognize that managing this transition effectively requires proactive policies focused on workforce training, education reform, and targeted support for displaced workers.

CHAPTER 3

AI AND THE BIG PURGE

"The most important social welfare program in America is a job."
– Newt Gingrich

As of January 2025, artificial intelligence (AI) had become the primary driver behind a seismic shift in the job market, triggering a techno-layoff phenomenon of mass displacement across diverse sectors. This chapter explores how AI continues to systematically purge employment opportunities, reshape the labor landscape— from government to tech roles, white-collar professions, and even simple blue-collar jobs.

AI: Big Purge on Employment

Artificial Intelligence is no longer merely augmenting human labor; it is actively replacing it. The first quarter of 2025 witnessed unprecedented layoffs directly attributable to AI integration:

- Over 172,000 job cuts were announced in February 2025, doubling the previous year's figures.
- More than 4,000 workers lost their jobs directly due to AI implementation since May 2024.

- Approximately 41% of companies now plan workforce reductions as AI capabilities expand.
- By 2030, nearly half (46.5%) of jobs in energy, utilities, and mining industries will be at high risk of automation.

Government Jobs: First on the Chopping Block

The public sector is at the forefront of this AI-driven displacement. The Department of Government Efficiency (DOGE) spearheaded by Elon Musk with the goal of shrinking the United States budget deficit by reducing government waste and fraud, launched an aggressive initiative to replace human labor with automated systems:

- Over 100,000 federal positions have already been eliminated under DOGE's initiatives.
- The Internal Revenue Service alone terminated 7,000 staff members.
- Agencies such as the Department of Defense, Environmental Protection Agency, and Veterans Affairs face significant reductions.
- In the UK, similar trends are evident as civil service staff numbers are almost certain to decrease significantly due to AI-driven efficiency drives.

This strategic shift toward automation in governmental roles aims to achieve productivity and efficiency savings estimated at billions of dollars annually. Routine administrative tasks—such as answering citizen inquiries or processing transactions—are increasingly managed by AI chatbots and automated platforms.

Tech Jobs: Accelerating Displacement by Industry Leaders

Google is reportedly preparing for a significant wave of layoffs, potentially affecting up to 30,000 employees, as it accelerates the integration of AI-driven tools and processes across its operations. This initiative aligns with the company's broader strategy to boost efficiency and streamline workflows through automation—a move reflecting governance practices increasingly seen in both private and public sectors.

The Details

- In December 2024, Google announced plans to restructure its ad sales department, signaling major organizational changes ahead.
- These rumored layoffs would follow the 12,000 job cuts earlier in 2024, which Google CEO Sundar Pichai described as necessary for adapting to shifting priorities and freeing resources for investments in emerging technologies.
- AI adoption is expected to transform critical areas such as ad sales operations and customer service roles, with automation reducing dependency on human labor.
- Job cuts also impacted Google's HR and Cloud units, further emphasizing the company's focus on reshaping its workforce to align with AI-driven strategies.

The Automotive Industry and Jobs Lost and Gained

The automotive industry has been undergoing a seismic transformation driven by artificial intelligence (AI) and autonomous technology since the mid-2010s. The U.S. automotive industry employs approximately 1.25 million people directly and 7.25 million indirectly, making it a cornerstone of the economy. However, the rise of autonomous vehicles threatens to displace up to 5 million jobs nationwide, including 3.5 million truck drivers and nearly all taxi drivers—roughly 3% of the U.S. workforce. These losses disproportionately affect workers in traditional roles, such as drivers, mechanics, and employees in internal combustion engine (ICE) manufacturing.

For example, consider a taxi driver who has spent decades navigating city streets, relying on their expertise to provide a livelihood for their family. With the advent of self-driving cars like Waymo's autonomous taxis, a taxi driver faces redundancy as AI systems take over their role. The widespread adoption of robotaxis not only eliminates these jobs but also creates challenges for displaced workers seeking employment nearby, as new opportunities often require specialized skills or are geographically inaccessible.

Way Mo' Problems, Jobs Lost & Gained

My experience on December 9, 2024 with a malfunctioning Waymo driverless vehicle serves as a compelling microcosm of the dual impact autonomous vehicles (AVs) have on the labor market: job losses for ordinary workers and job creation for highly skilled individuals. While AV technology is still a work in progress, its disruptive effects on employment are undeniable. While the service is still a work in progress, human drivers are replaced. The new skills needed to work for Waymo ride sharing services require particular skills. To work at Waymo, employees are required to have a diverse skill set tailored to the demands of autonomous vehicle technology. Proficiency in programming languages such as Python and C++ is critical for developing AI systems, alongside expertise in data analysis and machine learning tools to interpret large-scale datasets and refine autonomous operations. Problem-solving skills are essential for navigating complex systems, debugging issues, and ensuring reliability. Cross-functional collaboration is equally important, as employees must communicate effectively across engineering, hardware, and operations teams to meet project milestones.

Finally, familiarity with autonomous driving technologies, including sensors, cameras, and simulation tools, is crucial for roles in system maintenance and fleet management. Together, these skills enable Waymo's employees to drive innovation in the rapidly evolving autonomous transportation industry.

The Trucking Industry in Transition: Automation, Job Losses, and Opportunities

The trucking industry is undergoing a profound transformation due to the rise of autonomous vehicles (AVs). While this shift promises increased efficiency and cost savings, it also poses significant challenges for millions of workers. The impact of automation is not uniform—it disproportionately affects certain demographics, such as white male truck drivers and communities of color, while simultaneously creating new opportunities for skilled workers. This section explores these dynamics, supported by data visualizations to highlight the disparities.

White Male Truck Drivers: A Workforce at Risk

White men have historically dominated the trucking industry, comprising 62% of the workforce in driving occupations. Trucking has provided stable, well-paying jobs for those without higher education, particularly in rural areas. However, automation threatens to disrupt this demographic more than any other.

Key Statistics:

- **94% of long-haul operator hours** could be automated if AV technology is fully deployed across the U.S., leaving many drivers without work.
- **3.5 million truck drivers** in the U.S. face potential displacement due to automation, with long-haul routes being the most vulnerable.

Workforce distribution among truck drivers

Demographic	Current % of Workforce	Projected Job Losses (%)
White Male Drivers	62%	High (70-90%)
Black Male Drivers	12%	Moderate (50-70%)
Hispanic Male Drivers	17%	Moderate (50-70%)

(Data source: Databird Journal)

Communities of Color: Disproportionate Impacts

While white male drivers will bear the brunt of job losses numerically, Black and Hispanic drivers are also at significant risk. Truck driving is one of the top occupations for men of color, offering wages that often exceed those available in other industries accessible without a college degree.

Key Statistics:

- Truck driving is the **#1 occupation for Black men** and the **second-most common for Hispanic men**.
- Automation could exacerbate existing economic inequalities, as displaced workers from these communities may lack access to retraining or alternative employment opportunities.

The Need for Skilled Employees Amid Transformation

While automation eliminates traditional roles like long-haul driving, it creates demand for new jobs requiring advanced technical skills. These roles include maintaining autonomous systems, managing logistics software, and overseeing fleet operations.

Key Opportunities:

- **Technician roles:** Maintaining sensors, cameras, and AI systems on autonomous trucks.
- **Logistics management:** Overseeing dispatch systems powered by AI.
- **Remote monitoring:** Supervising fleets of autonomous vehicles from centralized hubs.

However, these opportunities often require specialized training or higher education—qualifications that many displaced truck drivers do not currently possess. Without significant investment in retraining programs, the gap between those who lose jobs and those who gain them will continue to widen.

Year	Traditional Driving Jobs Lost	New Tech-Based Jobs Created
2025	100,000	20,000
2030	500,000	150,000
2035	1 Million	400,000

The Concern

Automation is reshaping the trucking industry at an unprecedented pace. White male truck drivers face significant displacement due to their dominance in traditional roles, while communities of color risk losing critical economic lifelines tied to driving jobs. At the same time, new opportunities are emerging for skilled workers who can adapt to technological advancements.

To navigate this transition responsibly:

- Policymakers must implement robust retraining programs targeted at vulnerable demographics.

- Companies should invest in upskilling initiatives to help displaced workers transition into tech-based roles.
- Public-private partnerships can ensure equitable access to emerging opportunities within the automated transportation sector.

The Need for Mitigation Strategies

The disparity between job losses and gains highlights the urgent need for proactive policies to support displaced workers. Governments must implement retraining programs, financial safety nets, and healthcare provisions to help affected individuals transition into new roles. Policymakers must also ensure transparency and accountability in emerging technologies to build trust among consumers.

My viral driving in circles experience with Waymo sparked global conversations about safety concerns and accountability in autonomous systems. It is imperative that we balance innovation with human oversight—a critical consideration as society navigates this unprecedented shift.

Pay Attention, Be Aware

The disruption caused by AI in transportation is both transformative and polarizing. While millions face job losses due to automation, new opportunities emerge for those equipped with specialized skills. I believe my experience inside a driverless Waymo vehicle is just a microcosm of this transition —highlighting both the challenges ordinary workers face and the potential for extraordinary individuals to thrive in an AI-driven economy. As governments and industries adapt to these changes, they must prioritize equitable solutions that empower all members of society to participate in the future of work.

Governance in the Private Sector

Google's 2024/2025 restructuring reflects a governance model that prioritizes agility and innovation, akin to practices common in private companies. Unlike public sector governance, which often involves regulatory oversight and stakeholder alignment, private-sector governance allows for streamlined decision-making and rapid implementation of strategic shifts. For example:

- Google's Public Sector division, created in 2024 operates as an independent entity, focusing on government clients while leveraging AI advancements like Gemini. This mirrors the flexibility seen in private-sector governance structures.
- The company's ability to adapt quickly—whether through layoffs or reorganizations—demonstrates its focus on aligning corporate strategy with emerging technologies without the constraints of public-sector transparency requirements.

Why It Matters

While Google continues to push AI innovations externally, it is aggressively applying the technology internally with profound workforce implications. This marks a pivotal moment in how artificial intelligence reshapes workplace dynamics—a trend set to intensify in 2025. Furthermore, Google's approach highlights the interplay between corporate governance models in private enterprises and public institutions. As AI-driven transformations accelerate across industries, companies like Google are setting a precedent for balancing efficiency gains with workforce restructuring—an approach that may influence both private and public sector strategies moving forward.

The tech industry exemplifies how rapidly AI-driven layoffs are occurring. Major corporations have aggressively adopted AI solutions to streamline operations and reduce human labor:

Company	Employees Laid Off (2025)
Meta	3,600
STMicro	3,000
Onsemi	2,400
Microsoft	2,280
Amazon	2,100
Workday	1,750
Cruise	1,050
Salesforce	1,000
eFishery	1,000
Blue Origin	1,000

These layoffs reflect a broader trend where entry-level and mid-level positions in technology firms are increasingly replaced by sophisticated AI systems capable of performing complex analytical tasks without human intervention.

White-Collar Recession: Professional Roles Under Siege

Historically immune to automation's impact, white-collar professions now face unprecedented vulnerability due to advancements in generative AI and machine learning. Positions once considered secure—such as financial analysts, junior lawyers, marketing strategists, HR associates—are disappearing rapidly. Termed the "White-Collar Recession," this phenomenon is characterized by a paradoxical economic environment where GDP rises while professional hiring sharply declines or ceases altogether.

The theoretical framework known as "Virtual Employee Economics" explains this phenomenon clearly: AI-driven efficiencies compound exponentially over time. Companies no longer view human labor as essential for growth but rather as a constraint limiting scalability and profitability.

Blue-Collar Jobs: Automation Revolutionizing Simple Tasks

Even traditionally secure blue-collar jobs are not immune from AI's reach. Automation is reshaping industries like fast food and retail:

- Domino's Pizza introduced autonomous delivery robots that could eliminate human drivers entirely.
- Pizza Hut developed robotic trucks capable of baking pizzas en route to customers.
- KFC launched a fully automated restaurant model drastically reducing human staffing requirements.

These examples illustrate how even straightforward manual tasks are vulnerable to automation through advanced robotics and AI integration.

Academia and Military: Specialized Roles at Risk

The academic sector faces disruption as generative AI tools automate research assistance roles previously held by junior researchers and administrative staff. Similarly, military modernization driven by advanced AI technologies automates routine logistical operations and maintenance tasks traditionally performed by personnel. Consequently:

- Routine military logistics and maintenance roles are increasingly automated.
- Combat operations are partially delegated to sophisticated autonomous systems.
- Overall troop numbers decrease while demand grows for highly specialized technicians proficient in operating advanced AI systems.

The AI Job Reckoning Spreads: From Government Offices to Fashion Runways

The disruptive force of AI is no longer confined to predictable sectors like manufacturing or data entry. As 2025 unfolds, even industries once considered immune to automation—government, fashion, entertainment, and education—are witnessing unprecedented workforce transformations.

Sectors Under Siege

1. **Government: 500,000 Federal Jobs at Risk**
   The Department of Government Efficiency (DOGE) plans to replace 500,000 federal roles with AI by 2030, targeting administrative, data processing, and customer service positions at agencies like the IRS and Social Security Administration. AI chatbots now handle 40% of routine inquiries, raising concerns about algorithmic bias and cybersecurity vulnerabilities.
2. **Tech: A Hiring Paradox**
   While demand for AI engineers and cybersecurity specialists surges (74% of employers struggle to find skilled workers), AI simultaneously automates coding, testing, and DevOps roles. Companies now use AI-powered platforms to screen 10,000 resumes/hour, displacing HR professionals.
3. **Education: Teachers vs. Tutors**
   AI's integration into classrooms threatens 14% of global education jobs by 2030. Tools like AI essay graders and virtual teaching assistants reduce demand for instructors, while universities face pressure to adopt "work-integrated learning" models that prioritize industry partnerships over traditional faculty roles.
4. **Fashion: The Rise of Digital Twins**
   H&M's deployment of 30 AI-generated models—which can "work" 24/7 without travel or fees—has

sparked industry-wide adoption. Brands like Balmain and Prada now use digital avatars for 60% of campaigns, displacing photographers, stylists, and makeup artists. The AI fashion market is projected to hit $1.77B in 2025, accelerating this shift.

5. **Entertainment: Hollywood's AI Takeover**
   AI now scripts, edits, and stars in films. Deepfake technology enabled Metaphysic's viral AI Tom Cruise videos, while studios use generative tools to cut VFX costs by 70%. The Animation Guild reports 25% fewer jobs in visual effects since 2023, with AI-generated movies like *Synthetica* (2025) threatening actors and directors [Hollywood Reporter].

Why This Matters: The Human Cost of Efficiency

- **Economic Polarization:** While AI could add $20T to the global economy by 2030, it risks concentrating wealth among tech elites. Fashion models and VFX artists face income drops of 40-60% as digital alternatives proliferate.
- **Creative Erosion:** AI's reliance on existing data stifles originality. H&M's AI designs are 89% derivative of past trends, risking homogenization.
- **Ethical Dilemmas:** Government AI systems trained on biased datasets have wrongly denied 12% of welfare claims, while deepfakes fuel misinformation crises.

Survival Strategies for the AI Era

For Workers:

- Upskill in AI Synergy: Fashion stylists learn 3D modeling; teachers master AI tutoring tools.
- Unionize: Hollywood's Animation Guild secured clauses limiting AI replacement in 2024 contracts [Hollywood Reporter].

For Industries:

- Hybrid Workflows: Luxury brand Chanel pairs human designers with AI tools, boosting productivity 30% without layoffs.
- Ethical Guardrails: The EU's AI Act mandates transparency in public-sector AI, a model for private industries.

For Governments:

- Job Transition Funds: Proposals for a 5% AI tax on companies to fund reskilling programs.
- IP Protections: Laws granting artists royalties when their work trains AI models, as seen in France's 2024 Copyright Reform.

The Bottom Line

AI's spread into creative and public sectors proves no job is truly safe. Yet history shows disruption breeds reinvention: just as ATMs expanded banking services, AI could democratize fashion design or streamline governance. The challenge lies in steering this transformation toward equity—not elimination.

Gender Disparities Intensify

AI-driven layoffs disproportionately affect women:

- Approximately 58.87 million women (8 out of every 10) work in occupations highly exposed to generative AI automation compared to only 48.62 million men (6 out of every 10).
- Women face a 21% higher risk than men for displacement due to automation.
- In tech specifically, women are currently 1.6 times more likely than men to experience layoffs.

The Writers' Strike Blueprint—How Hollywood Fought Back

The 2023 Hollywood writers' strike marked a watershed moment in labor's battle against AI displacement, offering both a cautionary tale and a roadmap for resistance. Over 11,500 Writers Guild of America (WGA) members halted production for 148 days to win historic protections against AI displacement—a victory with ripple effects across industries.

The AI Threat to Creative Careers

Writers like Danny Tolli and Leah Folta—once insulated by the "uniquely human" nature of storytelling—found their $136,690-average jobs at risk as studios explored AI for:

- Script generation: ChatGPT 4 could draft plot outlines and dialogue, threatening entry-level "staff writer" roles ($4,362/week).
- Rewrites: Studios proposed using AI for revisions to avoid paying writers residuals (post-air royalties).
- Training data: Unregulated use of existing scripts to train AI models, risking intellectual property theft.

The strike exposed how even high-skill creative roles face automation:

"ChatGPT 6 might do an even better job... It's scary." – Danny Tolli, TV writer.

The WGA's Historic Contract: Key AI Protections

The September 2023 agreement set critical precedents:

Protection	Impact
AI cannot write or rewrite scripts	Prevents replacement of human writers
Studios must disclose AI use	Transparency in creative process
Writers retain credit/compensation for AI-assisted work	Ensures fair pay
No requirement to use AI tools	Preserves creative autonomy

This contract became a model for labor negotiations, proving unions could shape AI integration rather than resist it entirely.

Broader Implications for the AI Workforce

The writers' victory offers lessons for other industries:

1. Collective Bargaining Works: 72% of Americans supported the strike, forcing studios to concede.
2. Early Intervention Matters: The WGA acted before AI became entrenched, unlike sectors like retail facing irreversible automation.
3. Hybrid Workflows Are Key: The deal allows AI as a tool (e.g., brainstorming), not a replacement—a template for fields like law and design.
4. However, challenges persist:
5. Training data loopholes: Studios can still use scripts to train AI unless legally challenged.
6. Global replication: Countries without strong unions (e.g., India's film industry) remain vulnerable.

Entertainment Job Disruption: 2025 Projections

Role	AI Exposure	Protections
Screenwriters	100%	WGA contract
VFX Artists	85%	None
Fashion Models (AI twins)	70%[CNN]	None
Federal Clerks	65%[DOGE plan]	Proposed AI tax

Pathways Forward: Beyond Hollywood

The WGA's success informs actionable strategies:

For Workers:

- Unionize: 25% of animation jobs saved through guild negotiations.
- Upskill in AI collaboration: Writers now learn prompt engineering to direct AI tools.

For Policymakers:

- Expand the WGA model: California's proposed SB-728 mandates AI transparency in all creative contracts.
- Fund reskilling: Redirect 5% of AI corporate profits to workforce programs (EU proposal).

For Corporations:

- Adopt ethical AI charters: Disney's "Human-in-the-Loop" policy requires 70% human creative control.

Writing the Future

The writers' strike proved that proactive resistance can steer AI's impact. As Tolli noted: *"We were the canary in the coal mine for all workers."* Their victory offers a script for surviving AI's next act—one where human creativity remains the star.

Looking Ahead: A Transformed Job Landscape

Projections for job displacement by the end of this decade are alarming:

- Globally, AI is projected to replace up to 800 million jobs by 2030.

- Over 120 million workers worldwide will require retraining within three years due to shifting industry demands driven by AI.
- In the United States alone, approximately 45 million jobs could be overtaken by artificial intelligence by the end of the decade.
- These changes could have a $15.7 trillion global economic impact by 2030.

Navigating an Uncertain Future

As we progress further into this transformative era marked by mass technological displacement across multiple sectors—including government roles previously considered secure—the implications become increasingly clear and starkly unavoidable. Traditional employment paradigms are rapidly eroding under pressure from relentless technological advancement powered primarily by artificial intelligence.

The challenge ahead lies not merely in retraining displaced workers but fundamentally reimagining employment itself within an economy dominated increasingly by machines rather than humans. The techno-layoff phenomenon represents not just another cyclical economic downturn but a profound structural shift demanding innovative policy responses capable of addressing unprecedented social disruptions caused by widespread job losses across government agencies, private businesses large and small alike—and even academia itself—as we enter deeper into an uncertain future shaped irrevocably by artificial intelligence technology.

CHAPTER 4

THE NEW ECONOMY - AI'S TRANSFORMATIVE ROLE

"The future belongs to those who can collaborate with AI, not compete against it."
– Demis Hassabis, CEO, Google DeepMind

We stand at the threshold of a new economic era, one driven not by traditional labor alone, but by autonomous, proactive digital entities known as **Agentic AI**. These intelligent agents are redefining productivity, reshaping industries, and fundamentally altering the nature of work. Just as the phrase "there's an app for that" once captured the essence of digital convenience, tomorrow's mantra will be: ***"There's an agent for that."***

Agentic AI: The Catalyst for Radical Disruption

Agentic AI systems differ radically from traditional automation tools. They are capable of independent reasoning, decision-making, and proactive task execution without continuous human oversight. Agentic AI is not merely assisting—it is actively managing complex workflows, coordinating across multiple platforms, and autonomously interacting with other agents to achieve goals efficiently.

This shift will disrupt virtually every sector:

- **For Students**: Traditional education must evolve rapidly. Students who master skills in AI management, agent training, and system oversight will find themselves in high demand. Courses in generative AI and agentic systems have already surged by over 1,000% in enrollment since 2023.
- **For Entrepreneurs**: Agentic AI dramatically lowers barriers to entry. Small and medium-sized enterprises (SMEs) can now scale rapidly without significant overhead costs by deploying digital workers that autonomously handle customer interactions, financial management, supply chain optimization, and strategic decision-making.
- **For Office Workers**: Routine tasks such as scheduling meetings, summarizing communications, conducting research, and managing projects are increasingly performed by autonomous agents. This frees human employees to concentrate on strategic thinking, innovation, and creative problem-solving.
- **For Manual Workers**: While physical tasks requiring complex spatial reasoning may remain human-centric longer than previously expected, manual roles will shift toward supervisory positions—overseeing and maintaining automated systems rather than performing repetitive labor directly.

Building the Company of Tomorrow—Today

The transformative power of Agentic AI means companies can operate with unprecedented efficiency using leaner teams. A new enterprise may require only:

Role	Responsibility
CEO	Strategic vision and direction
Creative Manager	Innovation and human-centric design
Assistant	Coordination between humans and AI systems
AI Agents	Autonomous execution of tasks across functions

This streamlined structure enables agility and rapid innovation. Businesses leveraging this model today will dominate tomorrow's markets.

The Rise of Digital Labor

Agentic AI unlocks a new economic model—one based on digital labor forces that operate continuously without fatigue or error. Salesforce CEO Marc Benioff describes this as "a new labor model, new productivity model, and a new economic model". Companies adopting agentic systems can significantly increase output without proportionally increasing headcount or operational costs.

A comparison illustrates this clearly:

Traditional Company Structure	Agentic Company Structure
Large teams with specialized human roles	Lean teams augmented by autonomous agents
High overhead costs (salaries, benefits)	Lower operational expenses
Limited scalability due to resource demands	Rapid scalability through digital labor

Agents Collaborating with Agents

One remarkable feature of this new economy is inter-agent communication. Autonomous agents don't just perform isolated tasks—they collaborate seamlessly with other agents to solve complex problems faster than ever before:

- **Supply Chain Management**: Agents autonomously coordinate logistics in real-time.
- **Customer Service**: Agents proactively resolve issues by communicating directly with other service providers' agents.
- **Business Intelligence**: Agents gather data from multiple sources autonomously to provide real-time analytics.

These interactions create a dynamic ecosystem where productivity multiplies exponentially.

The Urgent Need for AI Specialists and Consultants

The rapid adoption of Agentic AI creates an urgent demand for specialists who understand these technologies deeply. Roles such as "AI Specialist," "AI Consultant," or "Agent Trainer" will become highly sought-after positions commanding premium salaries. Businesses urgently need professionals who can:

- Implement and manage agent-based systems effectively.
- Ensure ethical deployment of autonomous technologies.
- Train staff on integrating human creativity with agent-driven efficiency.

Now is the critical moment to acquire these skills—those who act today will lead tomorrow's economy.

Agentic AI Adoption Trends (2022–2025)

Year	Adoption Level	Key Developments
2022	Early Exploration	Limited use cases; mainly text-based assistants
2023	Initial Integration	Generative AI breakthroughs (ChatGPT), early agent prototypes
2024	Rapid Expansion	Major platforms launch dedicated agentic services (Salesforce Agentforce, Microsoft Copilot)
2025	Mainstream Adoption	Widespread enterprise deployment; multimodal agents; inter-agent communication standardization

(Adapted from McKinsey & ZDNet reports)

A Defining Moment in Work History

The emergence of Agentic AI represents a defining moment—one that will reshape our very definition of work itself. Just as steam engines once moved workers from fields to factories during the Industrial Revolution, autonomous agents now move us from traditional workplaces into digitally augmented environments. **This transformation is not merely technological; it is economic, social, and cultural.**

The time to adapt is now. Whether you're a student preparing for your future career path or an entrepreneur building tomorrow's enterprise today—embrace the power of Agentic AI. Master these tools, become a specialist or consultant guiding others through this transition, and position yourself at the forefront of this revolutionary shift.

Once we said confidently: *"There's an app for that."* Now we say boldly: **"There's an agent for that."**

The AI revolution has begun—and it will redefine what we call work forever.

CHAPTER 5

THE CONTENT CREATOR ECONOMY: A GLOBAL GOLDMINE FOR THE FUTURE OF WORK

"Today everyone is a brand, media, and publisher."
– Mike Johns

The global economic landscape is undergoing a significant transformation, characterized by the burgeoning Content Creator Economy. This sector, projected to reach a valuation of $528.39 billion by 2029 with a Compound Annual Growth Rate (CAGR) of 22.5% from 2023 to 2030, represents more than just a financial upswing; it embodies a fundamental shift in labor dynamics, marked by unprecedented accessibility, empowerment, and the democratization of opportunities for traditionally marginalized communities.

The Smartphone Revolution: Democratizing Access and Participation

The widespread adoption of smartphone technology has functioned as a critical catalyst, disrupting conventional barriers to entry within the media and entertainment industries. This democratization of technology has fostered an environment wherein individuals, irrespective of socioeconomic status, geographic location, or demographic affiliation, can actively engage in content creation and dissemination. The smartphone, in this context, serves as a versatile and multifunctional tool, effectively integrating the functions of a television studio, recording booth, and publishing platform into a single, readily accessible device.

Artificial Intelligence: Augmenting Creativity and Efficiency

Contrary to prevailing anxieties surrounding technological unemployment, Artificial Intelligence (AI) is demonstrating a propensity to augment human capabilities within the realm of content creation. Rather than supplanting human creators, AI serves as a facilitative instrument, streamlining workflows, enhancing creative ideation, and optimizing audience engagement. Empirical evidence suggests that a significant proportion of content creators are actively solicited by brands to integrate generative AI into their content strategies (56%), with the overwhelming majority of AI adopters reporting positive reception from their respective audiences (71%). This demonstrates AI's potential to increase efficiency and expand creative possibilities within the sector.

Empowerment and Equity: Opportunities for Marginalized Communities

The Content Creator Economy possesses the capacity to foster empowerment and equity among traditionally marginalized groups, including but not limited to:

- **Teenage and Young Adult Females:** The creator economy provides a platform for teenage and young adult females to express their perspectives, challenge societal norms, and navigate conventional gender roles. This empowerment is facilitated by the relative autonomy and creative freedom afforded within the digital sphere. Moreover, the ability to monetize content related to beauty, lifestyle, fashion, and social commentary provides avenues for economic self-sufficiency and entrepreneurial endeavors.
- **Hip Hop Community:** The hip hop community, historically marginalized within traditional media outlets, finds in the content creator economy a space for authentic self-representation and economic self-determination. This medium allows artists, musicians, and cultural influencers within the hip hop sphere to bypass conventional gatekeepers, directly engage their fan base, and monetize their unique cultural capital.
- **Elimination of Economic Barriers:** A salient characteristic of the content creator economy is its capacity to mitigate economic barriers that typically impede access to traditional employment opportunities. The minimal capital investment required (i.e., a smartphone and internet access) renders content creation a viable economic activity for individuals residing in underserved communities or facing financial constraints. This promotes greater economic inclusion and fosters a more diverse and representative workforce.

Shifting Paradigms in Brand Building and Marketing Strategies

The ascendancy of the content creator economy has instigated a fundamental realignment of brand building and marketing strategies. Traditional advertising paradigms are gradually ceding ground to more authentic, creator-driven content initiatives. A discernible paradigm shift is evident as brands increasingly recognize the value of engaging with content creators to establish genuine connections with target demographics, leveraging the creators' pre-existing rapport, credibility, and influence within their respective communities. This move towards more organic and personalized marketing strategies underscores the growing significance of the creator economy within the broader business landscape.

Towards a More Equitable and Inclusive Future of Work

The Content Creator Economy is emblematic of a transformative shift in the landscape of labor, facilitating unprecedented opportunities for economic participation, self-expression, and empowerment. This model holds considerable promise for mitigating historical disparities and promoting a more equitable and inclusive future of work, if policymakers, industry stakeholders, and educational institutions collaborate to ensure equitable access, sustainable practices, and responsible technological integration. Further research is warranted to explore the long-term socioeconomic impacts of the creator economy and to develop strategies for maximizing its potential as a force for positive social change.

Projected Growth of the Content Creator Economy (2023-2029)

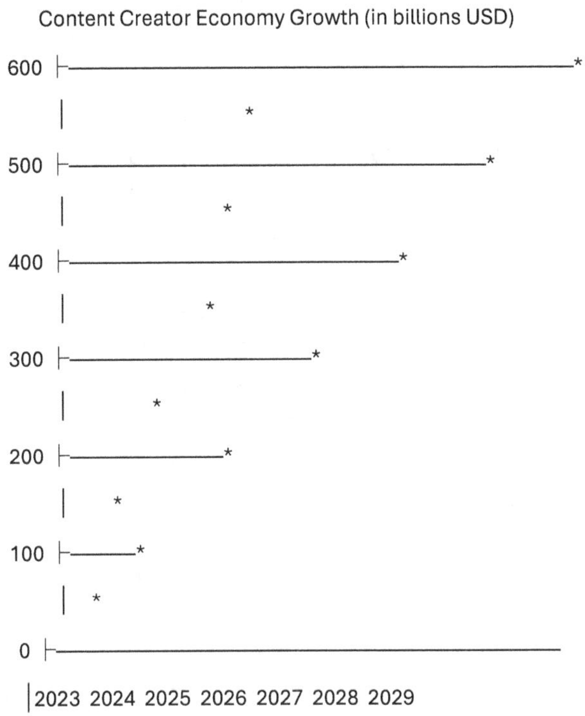

(Data source: The Business Research Company)

The Rise of the Creator Economy: Redefining Work in the Digital Age

The traditional concept of work is undergoing a radical transformation, driven by the explosive growth of the creator economy. This shift is reshaping not only how we view careers but also how education and businesses adapt to this new paradigm. The creator economy represents a democratization of work, where anyone with a smartphone and an internet connection can potentially build a career as a content creator or influencer.

The Allure of Influencer Careers

Recent studies have revealed a striking trend among Generation Z: one in four American kids now aspire to become social media influencers. This shift in career aspirations reflects the changing landscape of work and the growing influence of digital platforms. The appeal is clear - the potential for creative expression, financial independence, and the ability to build a personal brand that resonates with millions.

However, the reality of the creator economy is more nuanced. While the top echelon of creators can earn substantial incomes, the majority operate in a highly competitive space with varying degrees of financial success. According to Linktree's 2024 Report, the creator landscape is stratified into five categories based on follower count:

- Recreational (0-1K followers): 23 million
- Semi-Pro (1-10K followers): 139 million
- Pro (10K-100K followers): 41 million
- Expert (100K-1M followers): 2 million
- Expert+ (1M+ followers): 2 million

This distribution highlights that while the barrier to entry is low, achieving significant success remains challenging. Only 12% of full-time creators earn $50,000 or more annually, while 46% earn less than $1,000 annually from their content.

The Scale of the Creator Economy

The creator economy has grown exponentially, with over 200 million people worldwide now identifying as creators. This massive workforce is reshaping industries and creating new economic opportunities. The global influencer market size has doubled since 2019, reaching $21 billion in 2023.

Platforms like YouTube and Instagram have become launchpads for creators. On YouTube, 35,000 channels boast over 1 million subscribers, while on Instagram, 3.32% of users have between 100,000 and 500,000 followers. These numbers illustrate the potential for reach and impact within the creator economy.

Education's Role in the Creator Economy

As the landscape of work evolves, educational institutions must adapt to prepare students for careers in the creator economy. Arizona State University (ASU), recognized as a #1 school for innovation, has taken pioneering steps in this direction. The Future of Work program at ASU, which I had the privilege of contributing to, aims to bridge the gap between traditional education and the skills required for success in the digital age.

This program recognizes that the path to a successful career no longer necessarily requires a traditional four-year degree. Instead, it focuses on developing skills crucial for content creation, digital marketing, and personal branding. By embracing this shift, ASU is preparing students for a future where being an influencer or content creator is a viable and respected career path.

The Broader Impact on Work Culture

The rise of the creator economy is not just changing individual career paths; it's reshaping entire industries. At the National Association of Broadcasters' Sip and Tell event, I had the opportunity to educate industry leaders on the power of social media influencers. Creators like MrBeast, Dharmann, and Airrack are not just content producers; they're redefining what it means to be a media personality and entrepreneur in the digital age.

This shift is forcing traditional media and entertainment companies to rethink their strategies and adapt to a world where individual creators can command audiences rivaling those of established networks. It's a democratization of media production and distribution that was unimaginable just a decade ago.

The Future of Work and the Creator Economy

As we look to the future, it's clear that the creator economy will play an increasingly significant role in shaping work culture and career opportunities. While not everyone will achieve the astronomical success of top influencers, the creator economy offers a spectrum of participation levels. From side hustles to full-time careers, individuals can engage with this new economy in ways that suit their skills, interests, and goals.

Educational institutions, businesses, and policymakers must recognize and adapt to this shift. This includes:

1. Developing curricula that teach digital literacy, content creation, and entrepreneurship skills.
2. Creating flexible work environments that accommodate side hustles and creative pursuits.
3. Establishing legal and ethical frameworks to protect creators and consumers in this new economy.
4. Encouraging innovation and experimentation within traditional industries to stay relevant in the creator-driven landscape.

The creator economy represents a fundamental shift in how we think about work, education, and personal branding. It offers unprecedented opportunities for individuals to turn their passions into careers, but it also presents challenges in terms of sustainability and scalability. As we move forward, embracing and harnessing the power of the creator economy will be crucial for individuals, institutions, and societies looking to thrive in the digital age.

By recognizing the potential of the creator economy and adapting our educational and business models accordingly, we can ensure that the future of work is more inclusive, creative, and dynamic than ever before.

CHAPTER 6

WOMEN AND AI: THE IMPACT IS REAL

"Our systems will only work for everyone if they are designed with multiple voices in the room, every step of the way."
– **Tulsee Doshi,** Sr. Director & Head of Product, Google

The rise of artificial intelligence (AI) is transforming the workforce, creating both opportunities and challenges for women. As automation and generative AI redefine industries, women face disproportionate risks of job displacement while remaining underrepresented in critical AI roles. This chapter explores the intersection of women and AI, highlighting the barriers, opportunities, and solutions to ensure gender equity in the future of work.

The Challenges Women Face in AI

1. **Underrepresentation in AI Roles**
   Women make up only 30% of the global AI workforce, with even fewer holding leadership positions—just 14% occupy senior executive roles. This lack of representation perpetuates systemic gender biases in

AI systems and limits diverse perspectives needed to design equitable technology.

2. **Job Displacement Risks**
   Women are disproportionately employed in roles susceptible to automation, such as administrative support and customer service. According to Deloitte, nearly 79% of jobs held by women are vulnerable to automation compared to 58% for men. Without targeted reskilling programs, these workers risk being left behind in the evolving economy.
3. **Bias in AI Systems**
   AI systems often reflect biases present in their training data, leading to discriminatory outcomes that disproportionately impact women. For example, biased algorithms have been shown to perpetuate inequities in hiring practices, healthcare access, and financial services.
4. **Adoption Gap**
   While women's adoption of generative AI tools is rapidly increasing—projected to equal or surpass men's by the end of 2025—trust issues remain. Women express less confidence than men in generative AI providers' ability to secure their data, limiting their engagement with these technologies.

Opportunities for Women in AI

Despite these challenges, AI offers significant opportunities for women if barriers are addressed:

1. **Reskilling and Upskilling**
   AI-driven platforms like Coursera and Udacity provide personalized learning paths that enable women to acquire high-demand skills such as data science, machine learning, and ethical AI development. Reskilling initiatives can prepare women for emerging roles in technology while mitigating job displacement risks.

2. **Leadership Development**
   Increasing female representation in leadership positions within AI is critical for addressing systemic biases. Studies show that diverse teams improve productivity, innovation, and profitability. Programs like Deloitte's Women in AI Accelerator aim to equip women with the skills needed to lead in an AI-driven world.
3. **AI as an Equalizer**
   AI has the potential to minimize gender bias in recruitment and promotions by focusing on skills rather than demographics. Additionally, generative AI tools can enhance productivity and streamline workflows, empowering women across industries.

NEET: A New American Problem for Women

The rise of NEETs (young people *Not in Employment, Education, or Training*) is an emerging crisis that intersects with the challenges faced by women in the workforce. In the U.S., nearly one in five young people falls into this category, with two-thirds being women. The NEET phenomenon exacerbates existing inequalities and limits economic growth.

Why NEET Matters

- Economic Impact: NEET youth contribute to economic loss due to underutilized potential.
- Social Consequences: Extended periods as NEET lead to reduced lifetime earnings and diminished employment prospects.
- Gender Disparities: Women NEETs face additional barriers such as caregiving responsibilities and systemic biases.

Solutions for NEET

1. **Targeted Education Programs**
   AI-powered platforms can provide accessible skill-building opportunities tailored to NEET youth. Personalized learning tools can guide them toward high-demand careers.
2. **Mentorship Initiatives**
   Programs like MentorHer match young women with mentors who can help them navigate career paths and build professional networks.
3. **Public-Private Partnerships**
   Collaboration between governments and businesses can create scalable solutions such as apprenticeship programs and subsidized training initiatives.

Solutions for Gender Equity in AI

To ensure that women thrive alongside AI rather than being displaced by it, organizations must take deliberate action:

1. **Inclusive Reskilling Programs**
   Investing in gender-inclusive training initiatives is essential for preparing women for high-growth roles such as data scientists or ethical AI specialists.
2. **Eliminating Bias in Algorithms**
   Diverse teams are better equipped to identify and address biases embedded in AI systems. Increasing female representation among developers is crucial for creating equitable technology.
3. **Promoting Work-Life Balance**
   AI-driven tools can support flexible work arrangements that benefit women juggling caregiving responsibilities.
4. **Building a Culture of Inclusion**
   Organizations must foster environments where diversity is celebrated at all levels—from entry-level positions to executive leadership.

Why This Matters

The integration of AI into the workforce is not just a technological shift—it's a societal transformation that will define the future of work for generations. Without proactive measures to address gender disparities, women risk being excluded from high-growth sectors while bearing disproportionate burdens from automation.

Women's inclusion in AI isn't just about equity—it's about innovation. Diverse perspectives lead to better-designed systems that benefit society as a whole. By addressing barriers through reskilling initiatives, mentorship programs, and inclusive policies, we can ensure that women play a central role in shaping the future of work.

Men, Women & The AI Workforce

Metric	Women (%)	Men (%)
Representation in Global AI Workforce	~30%	~70%
Vulnerability to Automation	~79%	~58%
Senior Executive Roles	~14%	Majority

(Data sources: Deloitte Insights & CNBC)

These statistics highlight why addressing gender disparities is essential—not just for fairness but for building a resilient workforce equipped for tomorrow's challenges. By empowering women through education, leadership opportunities, and equitable policies, we can unlock their full potential in an era defined by artificial intelligence.

CHAPTER 7

DESKILL, UPSKILL, RESKILL, BE SKILLED

"Anything that a remote worker can do, AI will do better."
- **Avital Balwit,** Chief of staff, Anthropic

The AI revolution is no longer a distant threat; it's a current reality, and its impact on the job market is undeniable. That's why I see deskilling, upskilling, reskilling and being skilled not as trends, but as necessary steps for workers and organizations to take. In this chapter, we explore how these concepts are evolving in the age of AI and why mastering them is essential to not just survive, but thrive in the future of

Understanding the Shifting Sands: What is Deskilling, Really?

Deskilling, as it traditionally understood, is the process where jobs become easier or require fewer skills, usually thanks to technology. But in the age of AI, deskilling takes on new dimensions. It's not just about simplifying tasks; it's about AI systems taking over entire job functions that once required years of human expertise.

The Multifaceted Impact of AI on Deskilling

Automation of Complex Tasks: AI can break down complicated jobs into smaller, repetitive tasks that require fewer skills. This can leave workers feeling like their expertise is no longer valued.

The Leveling Effect: Certain AI applications help novices perform at levels closer to experts. While this sounds good in theory, it can diminish the value of years of experience and specialized training.

Reduced Cognitive Engagement: Over-reliance on AI tools can lead to a decline in critical thinking and decision-making abilities. Workers may become overly dependent on AI, losing their ability to solve problems independently.

It matters to you: it is crucial for staying with the times, for example with AI, if the jobs that are high in demand, then this leads to be a way to better your life with reskilling and upskilling. This allows the individuals to avoid the risk of "awkwardness" in the job market and allows the risk of deskilling to be less impactful.

Generational Divides: Deskilling's Uneven Impact

Age plays a significant role in how workers experience deskilling:

- **Older Workers:** They may struggle to adapt to new technologies, leading to a faster rate of deskilling in the roles they currently fill.
- **Mid-Career Professionals:** Often, their skills become obsolete quicker.
- **Younger Workers:** While they may find it easier to adapt to new technologies, they have limited opportunities to develop deep expertise in certain areas.

Gender Dynamics: Addressing Historical Inequities

The impact of deskilling isn't gender-neutral:

- **Occupational Segregation:** If certain jobs are being held by one gender, this can have a disproportionality.
- **Skill Recognition:** Skills traditionally associated with one gender may be undervalued in the AI-driven workplace.
- **Reskilling Opportunities:** Access to the new technology may be unequal.

The Dynamic Duo: Upskilling and Reskilling for the Win

To combat the threat of deskilling, individuals and organizations must prioritize upskilling and reskilling:

- **Upskilling:** Upskilling can be defined as focusing on existing skills to adapt to new technologies and work processes.
- **Reskilling:** Reskilling means to completely transition into different roles or industries.

Navigating the Path Forward: Strategies for Success

Focus on Skills That Complement AI: Develop expertise in areas like strategic thinking, emotional intelligence, creativity, and complex problem-solving.

Embrace Continuous Learning: Invest in learning programs that help you learn more on the landscape of AI.

To ensure that one is well-skilled, organizations and individuals must begin thinking strategically–now.

The New Standard: "Be Skilled" or Become "Obsolete"

We've talked about deskilling, upskilling, and reskilling, but let's be real: these are just steps on a longer journey. The real destination is a mindset, a commitment to becoming, and remaining, highly skilled. "Be Skilled" encapsulates what it truly means to thrive, not just survive, in the rapidly evolving digital world.

What Does it Mean to "Be Skilled"?

It's Not Just About Having Skills: It's about having a passion for learning, a dedication to mastery, and a willingness to adapt as new challenges arise. "Be skilled" means one knows how to learn and keep learning.

It's More Than a Job Title: Someone who is "skilled" isn't necessarily defined by their job description or their formal education. It's about the depth of their expertise, their ability to solve complex problems, and their commitment to excellence in their chosen field.

It's Not a Destination, but a Journey: "Be Skilled" isn't a one-time achievement; it's an ongoing commitment. It requires continuous learning, experimentation, and a willingness to embrace new technologies and techniques.

The Economic Imperative: Skilled = Value

In the AI-driven economy, skills are the new currency. Those who possess in-demand expertise will command higher salaries, enjoy greater job security, and have access to more opportunities for advancement.

- **Increased Earning Potential:** Skilled workers are more productive and can generate more value for their employers, justifying higher wages.
- **Greater Job Security:** As AI automates routine tasks, the demand for workers with specialized skills and problem-solving abilities will increase.
- **More Career Opportunities:** Skilled workers have more options, allowing them to pursue their passions and shape their careers.

The "Obsolete" Alternative: The Price of Complacency

Those who neglect to upskill and reskill risk becoming part of "The Obsoletes"— the segment of the population ill-equipped to compete in the modern job market.

The consequences of joining the ranks of "The Obsoletes" are dire:

- **Job Insecurity:** A shrinking pool of low-skill jobs increases competition and vulnerability to automation.
- **Wage Stagnation:** Without specialized expertise, workers are limited to entry-level positions with little room for advancement.
- **Social Marginalization**: A lack of relevant skills can lead to feelings of isolation, reduced social mobility, and a sense of being left behind.

The "Obsolete" demographic faces significant challenges in a society increasingly reliant on digital skills. They risk being left behind, both economically and socially.

Societal Impact: A Skilled Workforce Drives Progress

A society that values and invests in skills is a society that is poised for success.

A skilled workforce drives:

- Innovation: Expertise and creative problem-solving are essential for developing new technologies and solutions to pressing global challenges.
- Economic Growth: Skilled workers boost productivity, attract investment, and fuel economic expansion.
- Social Progress: A well-skilled population is more adaptable, resilient, and engaged in civic life.

The Time is Now: Seize the Opportunity

The AI revolution may seem daunting, but it also presents a unique opportunity to transform your career and your life. By embracing the "Be Skilled" mindset, you can:

- **Take Control of Your Future:** Don't let technology dictate your career path. Actively acquire new skills and shape your professional journey.
- **Find Meaningful Work:** Explore your passions, develop expertise in areas that excite you, and find work that is both fulfilling and economically rewarding.
- **Contribute to a Better World:** Use your skills to solve complex problems, drive innovation, and create a more sustainable and equitable future.

The bottom line? In the age of AI, "Be Skilled" isn't just a suggestion; it's a necessity. It's your shield against economic displacement, your key to career success, and your ticket to shaping a better future. It's time to commit to lifelong learning and unlock your full potential and to create a safety net for those who chose not to embrace or be part of this movement. Don't be awkward, it's your choice.

Level Up With AI: ***Resources and a Plan***

If you're ready to embrace the "Be Skilled" mindset, here's a starting point to level up your skills and take advantage of AI:

Identify your skill gaps:

Assessment Tools: Start by evaluating your current skill set and identifying areas for improvement.

Consider these areas:

- data literacy
- ability to do creative work

Set clear learning objectives:

Define Specific Goals: Where do you want to be in 1 year, 3 years, or 5 years?

Consider these areas:

- AI Prompt Engineering

- AI Consultant
- AI project management

Here are starting points:

- Coursera
- edX
- Udacity

Use AI to Accelerate Learning:

- AI learning platforms for personalized career planning and job search.

Stay Current:

- Follow reputable tech blogs, industry publications, and thought leaders on social media to stay informed about the latest AI trends and job market demands.

Assess Program Quality:

- Accreditation and Recognition: Look for programs that are accredited by reputable organizations or recognized by industry leaders.
- Curriculum Relevance: Ensure that the curriculum is up-to-date and relevant to current job market demands.
- Instructor Expertise: Check the qualifications and experience of the instructors. Are they experts in their field with a proven track record of success?
- Career Support: Does the program offer career counseling, job placement assistance, or networking opportunities?
- Cost and Financing Options: Compare the cost of different programs and explore financing options such as scholarships, grants, or loans.

The NEET Crisis: A Growing American Problem

NEETs (Not in Education, Employment, or Training) young people aged 15–24, represent a significant challenge for the future workforce. In the U.S., the number of NEETs has surged due to economic uncertainty, educational barriers, and a lack of accessible job opportunities. Globally, one in five young people (20.4%) falls into this category, with two-thirds of NEETs being women.

The Problem

1. **Economic Impact**: NEET youth contribute to economic loss due to underutilized potential. Their absence from the workforce affects GDP growth and increases reliance on social welfare programs.
2. **Social Consequences**: Extended periods as NEET can lead to "scarring" effects—reduced lifetime earnings and diminished employment prospects—which perpetuate cycles of poverty.
3. **Workforce Challenges**: Industries facing critical skills shortages in technology, healthcare, and renewable energy miss out on untapped talent that could fill these gaps.

Solutions to Empower NEET Youth

To address the NEET crisis and prepare workers for an AI-driven economy, targeted initiatives must focus on reskilling and creating pathways into meaningful employment:

1. Invest in Reskilling Programs

Organizations must prioritize training programs aligned with industry demands. For example:

- Programs like Amazon's retraining initiative for warehouse workers transitioning into IT roles.
- Generation's global employment programs, which provide hands-on training tailored to employer needs.

2. Expand Access to Education

Accessible education is key to reducing NEET rates. Digital learning platforms can provide affordable training opportunities for youth in underserved areas.

3 . Leverage AI for Workforce Development

AI-powered tools can identify skills gaps and recommend personalized learning paths for individuals based on their career goals.

4. Strengthen Public-Private Partnerships

Collaboration between governments, nonprofits, and businesses can create scalable solutions that address both immediate needs and long-term workforce challenges.

Why This Matters Now

The rise of NEETs highlights a critical missed opportunity for society—not just in terms of individual hardship but also in untapped economic potential. Addressing this issue is essential for building a resilient workforce that can thrive in an era dominated by AI and automation.

For women especially, who make up two-thirds of global NEETs, targeted interventions are vital to ensuring they are not left behind in this transition era. By investing in reskilling programs and creating equitable pathways into high-growth industries like technology and healthcare, we can turn this challenge into an opportunity—unlocking innovation, reducing inequality, and driving economic growth.

The rate of NEET growth among Men and Women

Metric	Women (%)	Men (%)
Global NEET Rate	~20%	~10%
Women as Share of NEETs	~67%	~33%
Skills Half-Life	36 months	36 months
Workforce Displacement by AI	~85M jobs	~85M jobs

(Data sources: CNBC, Deloitte Analytics)

These insights underscore why reskilling initiatives must be prioritized—not just as a response to technological change but as a solution to systemic inequities affecting women and youth globally.

Deskill, Reskill, Be Skilled

The future of work demands adaptability—not just from individuals but from organizations and governments alike. As AI reshapes industries at an unprecedented pace, continuous learning will be essential for survival in the workforce. At the same time, addressing the NEET crisis requires bold action to ensure that young people—especially women—are equipped with the skills they need to succeed.

By embracing reskilling initiatives and investing in youth-focused programs, we can transform untapped potential into thriving talent pipelines that fuel innovation across sectors. The stakes are high—but so are the rewards if we act decisively today.

CHAPTER 8

GENERATIVE AI AND THE REMAKING OF WORK

"Software that can think and learn will do more and more of the work that people now do. Even more power will shift from labor to capital."
– **Sam Altman,** Open AI Moores Law of Everything

Generative AI is rewriting the rules of work. As we barrel towards 2030, the impact of this technology will be even more profound, not only changing *what* we do, but *how* we do it, and even *why* we do it. Let's unpack what that looks like.

The AI Disruption: More Than Just Automation

Unlike previous technologies that primarily automated routine tasks, generative AI is coming for almost everyone. According to the Brookings Institute, at least 30% of all workers could see up to 50% of their current job roles change. In an interview on 60 Minutes, AI expert Kai-Fu Lee, has stated that AI could displace 40% of global jobs by the mid 2030s.

Skills in Demand: The New Human-AI Equation

- **AI Literacy:** By 2030, basic AI literacy won't be a niche skill; it'll be a baseline requirement for most jobs. Think of it like computer literacy in the early 2000s – if you didn't know your way around a computer, you were at a disadvantage. The same will be true for AI. This doesn't mean everyone needs to be a coder, but everyone needs to understand how to interact with and leverage AI tools effectively.
- **Fusion Skills:** "Fusion skills" are essential. Professionals who can intelligently interrogate AI systems, integrate AI outputs into decision-making, and learn alongside AI will be in high demand.
- **Human Skills:** Creativity, complex problem-solving, leadership, emotional intelligence – these uniquely human capabilities will become even more valuable. AI may handle data analysis and routine tasks, but it's up to us to provide the vision, empathy, and critical thinking that algorithms can't replicate.
- **Broader Skill Sets:** It isn't enough to have just a few skills. The most successful workers will be the ones expanding their skill sets.

The Transformation of Industries: From Legal to Retail and BeyondBy 2028, every industry will feel the transformative impact of generative AI:

- Legal, Banking, Insurance, and Capital Markets: expect massive transformation. AI will automate routine tasks, streamline processes, and drive innovation. However, human expertise will still be needed for complex legal interpretations, strategic financial decisions, and ethical considerations.
- Retail, Travel, Health, and Energy: will be reshaped by AI-powered personalization, automation, and optimization. Human workers will need to adapt to new

roles that require creativity, problem-solving, and customer engagement.
- And it goes beyond that, every sector is expected to be impacted by AI.

The Dawn of the Augmented Workforce: What Will Work Look Like?

Here's my vision for what work will look like in 2029:

- **AI-Augmented Roles:** AI will handle repetitive tasks, allowing humans to focus on creativity, strategy, and building relationships. I see the AI assistant becoming as commonplace as the personal computer.
- **Project-Based Work:** Instead of traditional jobs, we'll see a rise in project-based work, where individuals with specialized skills assemble teams to tackle specific projects. AI will help to manage these teams, automate tasks, and ensure efficient collaboration.
- **Remote Collaboration:** Enhanced by AI-powered translation tools and virtual collaboration platforms, teams will work together from anywhere in the world. This will create new opportunities for cross-cultural exchange and innovation.
- **Continuous Learning:** The pace of technological change will demand that workers commit to lifelong learning. AI-powered learning platforms will provide personalized training and upskilling opportunities, enabling individuals to stay ahead of the curve.

Navigating the Transition: It Starts Now

The transition to an AI-driven economy requires proactive measures from individuals and organizations:

- Upskilling and Reskilling: Workers must invest in acquiring new skills, particularly in areas like AI literacy, data analysis, and creative problem-solving.
- Organizational Adaptability: Companies must embrace AI and provide workers with the tools and train-

ing they need to succeed in this new environment. This also includes, importantly to provide support and care to those who are displaced.

- Re-Engineering the Mindset - a shift to lifelong learning will be a must.

The Rise of AI Agents and the End of Routine Work

The world of work is undergoing a seismic shift, driven by the rapid adoption of artificial intelligence (AI). Across industries, jobs characterized by routine and repetitive tasks are increasingly being replaced by AI agents. This transformation is not just a possibility, it is already unfolding, reshaping the workforce and redefining the concept of employment.

The Role of AI Agents in Government and Beyond

AI agents are at the forefront of this revolution. In government, they are being deployed to streamline processes, enhance efficiency, and reduce costs. For instance, AI tools can now analyze legal documents, process tariffs, and even provide customer service through intelligent chatbots. These agents are capable of handling tasks that once required human intervention, such as responding to routine queries or managing administrative workflows.

According to the World Economic Forum's *Future of Jobs Report 2025*, AI and related technologies will create 19 million jobs while displacing 9 million over the next five years. This dual effect highlights the transformative potential of AI: it not only replaces certain roles but also creates new opportunities in areas requiring advanced technological skills.

Job Displacement: The Numbers Behind the Trend

The impact of AI on employment is staggering. Recent studies predict that up to **300 million jobs worldwide** could be lost or significantly altered due to AI by 2030. In advanced economies like the United States and Europe, this represents nearly 9% of all jobs. Industries most affected include manufacturing, data entry, customer service, and administrative roles—fields heavily reliant on routine tasks.

The chart below illustrates the projected job losses across key sectors due to AI-driven automation.

Project Job Losses Due to AI-Driven Automation

Sector	Jobs Lost (2023-2030)
Data Entry Clerks	8 million
Administrative Secretaries	6 million
Accountants & Bookkeepers	4.75 million
Manufacturing Workers	2 million

(Data Source: World Economic Forum & McKinsey Reports)

In May 2023, over **3,900 U.S. jobs were directly attributed to AI-related layoffs**, making AI the seventh-largest contributor to job displacement that month. These numbers underscore a growing trend: jobs with predictable workflows are increasingly vulnerable to automation.

The Broader Implications for Workforce Dynamics

While job losses dominate headlines, it's important to recognize that AI is also creating opportunities. The demand for roles requiring technological proficiency—such as AI-driven data analysis, cybersecurity expertise, and programming—is surging. Workers with these skills are better positioned to adapt to the changing landscape.

However, this transition comes with challenges. A McKinsey study estimates that **120 million workers globally will need retraining** in the next three years to meet new industry demands. Without proactive reskilling initiatives, many displaced workers may struggle to find their footing in an increasingly automated economy.

A Gradual Shift or Sudden Disruption?

The adoption of AI follows a "gradually then suddenly" pattern. While initial implementation may seem slow, advancements in generative AI—capable of creating text, images, and even software—are accelerating this shift. By 2030, generative AI alone could automate nearly **30% of work activities** in the U.S., up from earlier estimates of 21%.

Preparing for an Uncertain Future

As we navigate this era of technological disruption, governments and businesses must act decisively. Policies promoting retraining programs, social safety nets for displaced workers, and ethical guidelines for AI deployment will be crucial. History has shown that technological revolutions often create more jobs than they destroy—but only if societies are prepared to manage the transition.

For workers in routine roles, the message is clear: adapt or risk becoming obsolete. Developing technological literacy and embracing lifelong learning will be essential for staying relevant in an AI-dominated world. On this point, a March 2025 Fortune Magazine article shared that China's six-year olds are being offered AI classes in school in an effort to train the next generation of tech CEOs and win thte global AI-wars.

In this unfolding narrative of automation and innovation, one thing is certain: the age of routine work is coming to an end. The rise of AI agents marks not just the *death of a job* but also the birth of a new era in human productivity.

CHAPTER 9

THE SYMBIOTIC RELATIONSHIP BETWEEN HUMAN-ROBOT AND COLLABORATIVE WORK

"In the realm of work, our robotic allies will begin as helpful partners, but beware: their efficiency may ultimately render your role obsolete."
– **Arnold Gordon-Bray,** Retired U.S. Army Brigadier General

As a futurist, I've always been drawn to the intersection of technology and humanity. I see the future not as a cold, sterile landscape dominated by machines, but as a vibrant, collaborative ecosystem where humans and technology work in concert to create something greater than either could achieve alone. That's why I believe the evolving relationship between humans and robots in the workplace, which some people find concerning, is not only natural but a promising evolution.

A History of Harmonious Progress: Echoes of Innovation

If we look back, it's clear that humans have always partnered with technology. It's not about replacing human labor; it's about augmenting human capabilities. That's why I see the integration of robots into the workforce as a natural progression. This isn't a sudden disruption; it's the next chapter in a story that stretches back to the invention of the wheel:

- The Wheel: It expanded our horizons, literally and figuratively, connecting communities and revolutionizing agriculture.
- The Printing Press: It democratized knowledge, fueling intellectual curiosity, progress, and even the Renaissance.
- The Automobile: It transformed personal mobility and reshaped our cities, giving individuals unprecedented freedom and convenience.
- The Mobile Phone: It created instant connections, putting the world's information at our fingertips and revolutionizing communication.

In each of these instances, there was an understandable initial apprehension. But as humans, we adapted. We integrated the new technology and reshaped our lives. Robots, then, aren't a threat. They are simply the most recent technological innovation on a timeline that has defined human civilization.

From Human-Mobile to Human-Robot: A Symbiotic Leap

Our existing relationship with technology, particularly the smartphone, makes the integration of robots a logical step:

- Human-Mobile: Our phones are extensions of ourselves, providing instant access to information, communication, and navigation.
- Wearable Technology: Devices track our health, enhancing our physical performance and providing personalized insights.

Building on this foundation, the introduction of robots into the workplace is about leveraging the best of both worlds:

- Human-Robot Collaboration: Robots are taking on repetitive, dangerous, and physically demanding tasks, freeing us to focus on higher-level responsibilities.

The Harmony of Efficiency and Well-being: Benefits of Collaboration

Let's be clear: this isn't about turning our workplaces into dystopian factories. It's about creating environments where technology empowers us to do more, to be more. The benefits are tangible:

- **Increased Efficiency:** Robots, tireless and precise, can boost productivity and output.
- **Improved Safety:** Hazardous tasks can be delegated to robots, protecting human workers from harm.
- **Enhanced Quality:** Consistency and precision improve the quality of goods and services.
- **Reduced Costs:** Resource optimization leads to savings and greater competitiveness.

Addressing the Concerns: A Bridge of Understanding

I recognize that the integration of robots raises understandable concerns. This isn't about ignoring the potential challenges; it's about finding solutions:

- **Job Displacement:** The fear that robots will replace human workers is real. That's why retraining and upskilling programs are essential.
- **Skill Requirements:** Acquiring the skills to work alongside robots can seem daunting. Accessible training initiatives are key.
- **Psychological Factors:** The anxiety and uncertainty surrounding robotic integration must be addressed with clear communication and empathy.

Weaving the Future: A Collaborative Symphony

What does this harmonious future look like? It's a future where uniquely human skills take center stage. Robots enhance our abilities, but they don't replace our core value:

- Humans provide: Creativity, innovation, emotional intelligence, critical thinking, and leadership.
- Robots provide: Automation, data analysis, physical assistance, and tireless precision.

Here's what I mean:

The Musician and the Synthesizer: The musician brings the emotion and composition, while the synthesizer provides a wider range of sounds and effects. It does not replace the musician, it makes the music richer.

The Architect and CAD software: The architect still provides the concept and design, while the software helps make the plan to scale easier and more accurate.

Seizing the Opportunity: A Call to Collaboration

The integration of robots isn't something to resist. It's something to embrace intelligently and thoughtfully. I urge businesses to:

- **Invest in training:** Equip workers with the skills they need to thrive in a roboticized workplace.
- **Foster collaboration:** Emphasize the partnership between humans and robots.
- **Communicate openly:** Build trust by addressing concerns and celebrating the benefits of this collaboration.

The Future is Collaborative

I firmly believe that the future of work is not about humans versus robots. It's about humans *with* robots. By combining our ingenuity, our empathy, and our critical thinking skills with the tireless precision and analytical power of machines, we can unlock unprecedented levels of productivity, innovation, and human well-being. Let's embrace this opportunity to compose a future where both humans and robots thrive. The key is for us to embrace this shift and not reject it.

CHAPTER 10

MEET THE OBSOLETES: THE TECHNOLOGICALLY DISPLACED

"You have disgraced the State before the masses. You have proven yourself a hypocrite, a traitor to the ideals of the State; you have, as such, no function. You are Obsolete!"
– ***The Twilight Zone,*** "The Obsolete Man"

Enter 2030, a distinct demographic is emerging – not defined by age, but by their relationship to technology. I call them "The Obsoletes." Unlike digital natives or the tech-savvy elite, these are individuals who, for various reasons, find themselves struggling to adapt to the rapidly changing, AI-driven job market. They're caught between eras, watching the world of work transform in ways that leave them feeling increasingly marginalized. This chapter delves into the realities faced by The Obsoletes, exploring the structural forces that contribute to their precarious position and proposing paths forward that foster inclusion and opportunity.

The Erosion of Traditional Pathways: The Shrinking Low-Skill Job Market

The Obsoletes are particularly vulnerable to the dramatic shifts occurring in the low-wage job market. By 2030, several key sectors will have undergone significant transformations:

- **The Fast Food Industry:** Once a reliable source of entry-level employment, this sector is experiencing rapid automation. Self-service kiosks, robotic burger flippers, and AI-powered order-taking systems are reducing the need for human workers, particularly in routine, customer-facing roles.
- **The Retail Sector:** The ongoing dominance of e-commerce, coupled with the rise of automated stores and cashier-less checkout systems, is leading to a decline in traditional retail positions. The Obsoletes who relied on these jobs for income and stability are finding fewer opportunities available.
- **The Manufacturing Sector:** Advanced robotics, AI-driven quality control, and automated production lines are transforming manufacturing, significantly reducing the demand for low-skill, manual labor. This trend is displacing workers who lack the skills and training to operate and maintain these advanced systems.

The Lingering Opportunities: Where Human Labor Still Matters

While AI and automation are reshaping the landscape of low-skill employment, certain sectors will continue to require human labor, at least for the foreseeable future. These remaining opportunities may become increasingly important for The Obsoletes:

- **Waste Management and Circular Economy:** As global waste production continues to escalate, innovative approaches to waste management and upcycling are gaining traction. This creates a need for workers skilled in waste data handling, sorting, and creative "garbage design" – finding innovative ways to reuse and repurpose waste materials.

- **Cleaning Services:** While routine cleaning tasks may be automated, many facilities will still require human cleaners for complex or delicate tasks, such as sanitizing sensitive equipment, maintaining historic buildings, or providing personalized cleaning services for high-end clients.
- **Urban and Vertical Farming:** The rise of vertical farming and the growing demand for locally-sourced, sustainable food production are creating opportunities for those willing to work in urban agriculture. These roles may involve planting, harvesting, and maintaining crops in indoor, controlled environments.

The Socioeconomic Realities: Challenges Faced by The Obsoletes

Despite the existence of these remaining opportunities, The Obsoletes face significant challenges in securing stable, well-paying employment:

- **Limited Job Prospects and Heightened Competition:** The dwindling number of low-skill jobs, coupled with an increasing pool of displaced workers, is creating fierce competition for available positions. This competition can lead to exploitation, depressed wages, and poor working conditions.
- **Wage Stagnation and Economic Insecurity:** Even with potential increases in the minimum wage, The Obsoletes may struggle to secure full-time employment or advance beyond entry-level positions. The lack of benefits, paid time off, and opportunities for career advancement contributes to economic insecurity and limits their ability to build wealth.
- **Social Stigma and Reduced Social Mobility:** In a society that increasingly values technological literacy

and adaptability, The Obsoletes may face discrimination, prejudice, and reduced opportunities for social and economic advancement. The perception that they are "falling behind" can lead to feelings of isolation, shame, and hopelessness.

The Path Forward: Strategies for Empowerment and Inclusion

The question is what can The Obsoletes do for themselves, not just what society should do for them. Here are strategies they can implement:

- **Embrace Micro-Upskilling:** Don't feel like you need a full degree to get ahead. Focus on acquiring specific, in-demand skills through short courses and online tutorials. Learn a new software program, master a particular social media platform, or become proficient in a niche skill related to the green economy or healthcare support.
- **Leverage Existing Skills in New Ways:** Think about how your current skills can be applied to emerging industries. If you're a skilled customer service representative, for example, explore opportunities to provide personalized support for AI-driven products or services. Or if you are interested in design, take a CAD program to stay ahead
- **Network Strategically:** Don't underestimate the power of networking. Attend local community events, connect with people in your field on social media, and seek out mentors who can provide guidance and support.
- **Explore the Creator Economy:** Turn your passion into a side hustle by creating content online. Whether it's writing, video production, or social media management, the creator economy offers opportunities to monetize your skills and build a personal brand.

- **Become a Problem Solver for Local Businesses:** Small businesses often struggle to keep up with the latest technological trends. Offer your services as a tech-savvy consultant or troubleshooter, helping them to navigate new software programs, set up online marketing campaigns, or streamline their operations.
- **Seek government resources to assist:** The government has retraining programs as well.

To address the challenges faced by The Obsoletes, as a society we must consider:

- **Targeted Retraining Programs:** Developing accessible upskilling initiatives focused on transitioning workers into growing fields like green technology and healthcare. As seen The last Bastions of Low-Skill Employment
- **Social Support Systems:** Implementing stronger safety nets to prevent The Obsoletes from falling into extreme poverty. For those who chose not to do it there has to be an ethical solution.
- **Redefining Work:** Exploring alternative economic models that value contributions beyond traditional employment, such as community service or environmental stewardship.
- **Universal Basic Income:** Would Universal Basic Income help address the impact of AI on human jobs? Is it an option for the government or hybrid of government along with the large corporations that utililzed human creativity to develop AI, automation and robotics, only to sever its human workforce to increase its corporate profits?

Addressing Systemic Inequities: A Focus on Racial and Ethnic Minorities

It's crucial to acknowledge that the challenges faced by The Obsoletes are often compounded by existing systemic inequities that disproportionately affect Black, Mexican, and other minority workers. These communities are at a higher risk of job displacement due to AI and automation, face greater barriers to accessing retraining opportunities, and are more likely to experience discrimination and exploitation in the labor market.

Therefore, addressing the needs of The Obsoletes requires a targeted approach that takes into account the specific challenges faced by minority communities. This could include:

- Investing in community-based organizations that provide culturally competent training and support services.
- Implementing affirmative action policies to promote equitable representation in high-growth industries.
- Addressing discriminatory practices in hiring, promotion, and wage determination.
- Ensuring equitable access to education and technology for all communities.

Creating a Future that Includes Everyone

The fate of The Obsoletes serves as a stark reminder that technological progress does not automatically translate into economic and social progress for all. It is our collective responsibility to ensure that the benefits of AI and automation are shared broadly and that those who are most vulnerable to displacement are provided with the support and opportunities they need to thrive.

By embracing a human-centered approach to workforce development, strengthening social safety nets, empowering The Obsoletes to take proactive steps, and addressing systemic inequities, we can create a future of work that is more inclusive, equitable, and sustainable for all members of society. Failing to do so risks creating a divided society, where a growing segment of the population is left behind by the forces of technological change.

CHAPTER 11

UNIVERSAL BASIC INCOME, MAYBE?

"I am now convinced that the simplest approach will prove to be the most effective — the solution to poverty is to abolish it directly by a now widely discussed measure: the guaranteed income."
– Dr. Martin Luther King Jr.

Imagine: We're on the cusp of 2030 and the rapid advancement of Artificial Intelligence and the evolution of work demand innovative solutions to address the growing economic and social disruptions. Two crucial considerations destined to gain prominence (as early as 2028) are the ethical governance of AI and the implementation of Universal Basic Income (UBI). This chapter explores the merits of UBI as a response to the challenges posed by AI and automation and examines its potential as a foundational component of a future workforce that embraces the advancements in technology.

The Evolving Landscape of Employment and UBI

The traditional model of full-time, stable employment is increasingly giving way to the gig economy, characterized by freelance, contract, and temporary work arrangements. This shift offers potential benefits in terms of flexibility and autonomy but also introduces significant precarity, including income instability and limited access to benefits.

Moreover, the automation of tasks previously performed by human workers, accelerated by AI and robotics, raises concerns about widespread job displacement and economic inequality.

In this dynamic environment, a UBI emerges as a proactive strategy for ensuring basic economic security for all citizens, regardless of employment status. UBI aims to provide a regular, unconditional cash payment to every member of society, offering a safety net that guarantees access to essential resources and enabling individuals to navigate the uncertainties of a rapidly changing labor market.

Andrew Yang– businessman, lawyer and former Presidential candidate and founder of the "Forward Party" frames UBI as a "Freedom Dividend." He has advocated UBI in the amount of $1,000 per month to every American adult, asserting that this unconditional income would help empower individuals to meet their basic needs, pursue education and training, launch businesses, engage in creative endeavors, and invest in their communities.

UBI: A Catalyst for Economic Growth, Innovation, and Social Well-being

Beyond serving as an economic safety net, UBI has the potential to stimulate economic growth and foster innovation. By injecting capital into the hands of consumers, UBI can increase demand, support small businesses, and stimulate job creation, particularly in local communities. Moreover, a guaranteed basic income can enable individuals to take calculated risks, pursue new ideas, and invest in their own human capital, thereby fostering a more dynamic and innovative economy.

Furthermore, UBI has the potential to promote social well-being by providing individuals with the time and resources to engage in activities that contribute to personal and societal betterment, such as caregiving, volunteering, artistic expression, and civic engagement. This reframing of "work" beyond traditional employment aligns with a growing emphasis on purpose-driven lives, where individuals prioritize personal fulfillment and social impact over purely economic considerations.

Addressing Potential Concerns and Charting a Pragmatic Path Forward

While the potential benefits of UBI are compelling, its implementation also entails a number of challenges that must be carefully considered and addressed. These challenges include:

- **Economic Feasibility:** Funding a UBI program on a large scale requires careful consideration of potential revenue sources, including reallocating existing welfare programs, implementing progressive tax policies, and capturing the economic gains from automation.
- **Work Incentives:** Concerns about potential disincentives to work must be addressed through careful program design and complementary policies that encourage labor force participation.
- **Implementation Challenges:** Designing an effective and equitable UBI system requires careful attention to payment levels, distribution mechanisms, and integration with existing social safety nets. The Brookings Institute suggests how this could be done with an ESG type fund.

Fortunately, real-world pilot programs are providing valuable insights into these challenges and informing the development of effective UBI models. These trials are demonstrating that UBI can be a viable and effective tool for promoting economic security and social well-being.

Addressing Concerns for the Technologically Averse: A Human-Centered Approach to Automation

As AI becomes more pervasive, it's crucial to recognize that not everyone embraces technological progress with open arms. Some individuals may harbor concerns about the ethical implications of AI, its potential to displace human workers, and its impact on privacy and autonomy.

A human-centered approach to automation requires:

- Ensuring that AI systems are designed and deployed in a manner that respects human values and promotes human well-being.
- Providing individuals with the opportunity to opt out of AI-driven systems and services, allowing them to maintain control over their own data and choices.
- Supporting individuals who may be displaced by automation with retraining programs and resources to transition to new careers.

UBI and Those "Not Participating:" Addressing the Question of Social Contribution

One particularly salient question surrounding UBI is how to address the concerns of those who may choose not to participate in the formal labor market, what I've described as "The Obsoletes." This encompasses individuals who, due to various circumstances, may not be engaged in traditional employment or entrepreneurial endeavors. It's worth noting that those choosing not to participate or who are not afforded the opportunities, should not be left out.

A UBI framework can be designed to:

- Recognize and value non-market contributions to society, such as caregiving, volunteer work, community engagement, and artistic expression.

- Encourage participation in civic activities and promote a sense of social responsibility.
- Promote a culture of lifelong learning and personal development, empowering individuals to acquire new skills and pursue their passions, regardless of employment status.

AI Governance: Ethical Frameworks and Oversight

Alongside UBI, the responsible governance of AI will be an increasingly critical issue. As AI systems become more pervasive and powerful, it it is essential that ethical frameworks and oversight mechanisms are established to ensure AI systems are used for good.

This includes:

- **Addressing Bias and Fairness:** Ensuring that AI systems are free from bias and do not perpetuate discrimination.
- **Promoting Transparency and Accountability:** Making AI decision-making processes transparent and holding developers accountable for the actions of their systems.
- **Safeguarding Privacy and Data Security:** Protecting individuals' privacy and ensuring that AI systems are used responsibly with sensitive data.
- **Managing Job Displacement:** Implementing policies to mitigate the negative impacts of automation on the workforce, such as retraining programs and support for displaced workers.

The Interplay Between UBI and AI Governance

UBI and AI governance are not mutually exclusive; rather, they are complementary strategies for navigating the challenges and opportunities of the future of work. UBI can provide a safety net for those displaced by AI-driven automation, while strong AI governance frameworks can ensure that these technologies are used responsibly and ethically.

UBI in 2028-2030– A Necessary Investment in Our Future?

As we look to the future, it's clear that UBI is not just a radical idea but a pragmatic solution to the challenges of the 21st century. By 2028-2030, the need for a safety net, a stimulus, and a redefinition of "work" will be more urgent than ever. By investing in UBI and implementing responsible AI governance frameworks, we can create a society that is more equitable.

As artificial intelligence (AI) transforms the workforce, governments face the challenge of ensuring that technological advancements benefit society without exacerbating inequality or unemployment. The concept of Universal Basic Income (UBI) has resurfaced as a potential solution to address these concerns. Here, we explore how UBI could play a role in the future of work scenario, where AI-driven automation is reshaping industries.

The Challenge of AI-Driven Automation

AI technologies, including those used in electric vehicles, autonomous vehicles, and robotics, are increasingly capable of performing tasks traditionally done by humans. This shift raises concerns about job displacement, particularly for workers in sectors where automation is most prevalent. For instance, autonomous vehicles could significantly reduce the need for human drivers, while AI in manufacturing could replace assembly line workers.

Universal Basic Income as a Potential Solution

UBI proposes providing every citizen with a guaranteed cash benefit, regardless of their employment status. This approach has been suggested as a means to ensure a minimum standard of living for those displaced by automation. Proponents argue that UBI could help mitigate the economic impacts of job loss and provide financial security during periods of transition.

However, critics point out that UBI could be extremely costly and might not effectively address inequality or promote economic mobility. For example, a UBI that pays $10,000 annually to every U.S. adult would require significant funding, potentially diverting resources from targeted programs that could better support those in need.

Alternative Approaches

Instead of UBI, some experts advocate for targeted measures that focus on upskilling workers and providing wage subsidies to low-income earners. These strategies aim to enhance human capital and encourage workforce participation, rather than solely relying on unconditional cash transfers.

Government Measures for the Future of Work

To address the challenges posed by AI-driven automation, governments should consider the following measures:

1. **Upskilling and Reskilling Programs**: Invest in education and training initiatives that help workers adapt to AI-driven changes in the job market.
2. **Targeted Income Support**: Implement wage subsidies and targeted transfer benefits to support low-income workers and those most affected by automation.
3. **Regulatory Frameworks**: Develop regulations that ensure AI systems are transparent, fair, and accountable, minimizing risks such as algorithmic bias.
4. **Social Safety Nets**: Strengthen existing social safety nets to provide a robust support system for those displaced by automation.
5. **Encouraging Responsible AI Adoption**: Promote the development and deployment of AI technologies that align with societal values and support economic growth without exacerbating inequality.
6. **Wage Insurance:** Implementing programs that partially compensate workers who take lower-paying

jobs after being displaced by AI, helping to maintain their income levels.

7. **Education Subsidies and Grants:** Providing financial support for workers to pursue further education or acquire new qualifications, enabling them to adapt to changing job markets.
8. **Targeted AI Taxes**: Implementing taxes on AI-driven profits or automation to fund social programs and job creation initiatives.

By adopting these strategies, governments can create a future where AI enhances productivity and economic opportunity without leaving workers behind. While UBI remains a topic of debate, it highlights the need for innovative solutions to address the challenges of the AI-driven future of work.

CHAPTER 12

CTRL+ALT+DEFEAT: THE GEN Z UPRISING AGAINST CORPORATE AI

"Ultimately, technology is just a tool.
People give it purpose."
– **Satya Nadella,** Chairman & CEO, Microsoft

How Young Workers Are Rewriting the Rules of Automation Resistance

The integration of artificial intelligence in the workplace has sparked a generational divide, with younger workers at the forefront of both adoption and resistance. This chapter explores the complex relationship between Gen Z, Millennials, and AI in the corporate world.

The Paradox of Digital Natives

Despite being labeled as "digital natives," Gen Z and Millennials exhibit a surprising level of anxiety about AI's impact on their careers. A survey by the educational technology company, D2L, found that 52% of Gen Z workers worried about being replaced by more AI-savvy employees, compared to just 33% of Gen X respondents. This concern is compounded by the fact that many young workers feel ill-equipped to navigate the evolving landscape of AI-driven workplaces.

The Resistance Toolkit

Young workers are not passively accepting the AI revolution. Instead, they're developing sophisticated tactics to push back:

1. **Data Poisoning**: Deliberately skewing training datasets with irrelevant or misleading inputs.
2. **Ghost Prompting**: Using AI tools like ChatGPT to generate compliance complaints about AI oversight.
3. **Synthetic Strikes**: Coordinating "error avalanches" via encrypted communication channels.

These tactics reflect a deep-seated anxiety about job security and a desire for more control over the implementation of AI in their work lives.

The Cybersecurity Conundrum

Paradoxically, while Gen Z and Millennials are at the forefront of AI resistance, they're also considered the "weak link" in cybersecurity. A survey by EY Cybersecurity solutions firm reveals that only 31% of Gen Z workers feel very confident in spotting phishing attempts, down from 40% in 2022. This vulnerability highlights the complex relationship young workers have with technology – embracing it in some areas while resisting it in others.

The Trust Dilemma

Interestingly, a study by Pearl.com found that 41% of Gen Zers trust AI more than humans, and 50% feel more comfortable confiding in AI about work issues than their managers. This preference for AI over human interaction in certain contexts adds another layer of complexity to the generational response to workplace automation.

The Adoption Gap

Despite their concerns, younger generations are leading the way in AI adoption at work. A Randstad USA survey found that 34% of Gen Z and 25% of Millennials engage with AI for various work tasks frequently, compared to much lower rates among Gen X and Boomers. This suggests that while young workers are wary of AI's impact, they're also at the forefront of leveraging its capabilities.

The Path Forward

To address these challenges, companies must:

1. **Invest in Training**: Only about half of Gen Z and Millennial workers report receiving AI training from their employers. Increasing this number could help alleviate fears and improve adoption.
2. **Promote Transparency**: Companies that share their automation roadmaps see significantly less resistance from employees.
3. **Encourage Participation**: Involving young workers in AI design and implementation can reduce sabotage and improve overall acceptance.

The Human Imperative in the AI Workplace Revolution

The Gen Z and Millennial response to AI in the workplace is multifaceted, blending anxiety, resistance, and adoption. These digital natives are not merely passive recipients of technological change—they are active participants, shaping how AI is integrated into their work environments. As artificial intelligence continues to reshape the job market, addressing their concerns will be crucial for successful implementation and the future of work itself. However, this is not just about adapting to technology; it's about redefining the relationship between humans and machines in a way that prioritizes trust, productivity, morale, and brand integrity.

Human-AI Focus vs. AI-Human Focus

Big companies must recognize that their approach to AI integration can make or break their workforce dynamics. A **human-AI focus**, where technology amplifies human skills and complements workers' contributions, is far more sustainable than an **AI-human focus**, which positions humans as secondary to machines. The latter risks alienating employees, eroding trust, and sparking rebellion—a trend already visible in workplace sabotage and public backlash against automation.

Key Human-AI Factors:

1. **Trust**: Workers who feel sidelined by AI systems are less likely to trust their employers. Trust is foundational for collaboration and innovation.
2. **Productivity**: While AI can streamline repetitive tasks, its misuse or overreach can lead to inefficiencies caused by resistance or errors.
3. **Morale**: When employees feel valued and empowered by technology, morale improves. Conversely, an AI-centric approach can lead to burnout and disengagement.
4. **Brand Image**: Companies that fail to prioritize human-centric AI risk reputational damage—both internally among employees and externally with consumers.

The Independent Movement: A Rebellion for Human Skills

The resistance led by Gen Z and Millennials against corporate AI overreach is one of the greatest signs of an independent movement centered on human skills. This rebellion isn't anti-technology; it's a demand for balance—a call for workplaces where humans remain at the core of decision-making processes.

Signs of Resistance

- **Sabotage Tactics**: From data poisoning to synthetic strikes, young workers are leveraging creative methods to disrupt AI systems they perceive as exploitative.
- **Public Backlash**: The vandalism against Waymo vehicles in cities like San Francisco and Los Angeles reflects broader societal concerns about automation replacing jobs.
- **Value-Driven Choices**: Gen Z workers prioritize mental health, flexible schedules, and purpose-driven roles—values that conflict with purely efficiency-driven AI systems.

These actions highlight a growing demand for workplaces that respect human ingenuity over algorithmic precision. As one anonymous worker put it: *"We're not fighting technology; we're fighting its misuse."*

Lessons for Big Companies

To avoid alienating their workforce or becoming the next cautionary tale (like Waymo's vandalized fleet), corporations must adopt proactive strategies:

- **Human-Centric Design**
  Involve employees in the design and implementation of AI systems. According to the Writer AI survey, 81% of workers would collaborate on AI initiatives if given the opportunity. This approach fosters trust and reduces resistance.
- **Transparency**
  Share automation roadmaps openly with employees. Companies that do so see 53% less sabotage. Transparency builds confidence in leadership intentions.
- **Upskilling Programs**
  Invest in robust training programs to help workers adapt to new technologies. Deloitte's 2024 survey found that over half of Gen Z workers believe reskill-

ing will be essential for navigating an AI-driven future.

- **Ethical Accountability**
  Ensure that AI systems are used responsibly. As Joe Amditi, Adjunct Professor from Montclair State University noted, *"AI tools should not be put in charge of decisions where accountability is required"*.

The Ripple Effects

Failure to adopt a human-AI focus could lead to significant consequences:

- **Economic Losses**: Resistance tactics like sabotage have already cost companies $300 million each year.
- **Turnover Rates**: Teams with unauthorized AI tool conflicts experience turnover rates 4.2 times higher.
- **Public Perception Damage**: Viral campaigns like #AIIsOverParty showcase how quickly public sentiment can turn against companies perceived as prioritizing machines over people.

Conversely, companies that embrace human-centric approaches report higher innovation output (92%) and stronger employee engagement.

The Road Ahead

The Gen Z/Millennial rebellion against corporate AI overreach is not just a workplace issue, it's a societal shift demanding accountability from big tech companies. This movement highlights the need for organizations to rethink their priorities as they integrate generative AI into their operations.

Why It Matters

For corporations, this rebellion serves as both a warning and an opportunity:

- It warns against adopting technology without considering its impact on people.

- It offers a chance to redefine innovation as a partnership between humans and machines.

By focusing on human skills rather than replacing them, companies can build workplaces that thrive in the age of automation while maintaining trust, morale, and productivity.

As one resistor aptly summarized: *"We'll crash your AI before it crashes our lives."* For big companies looking ahead, this sentiment should serve as a wake-up call—because the future of work belongs not just to machines but also to the humans who wield them.

"Machines compute; humans create. The future belongs to balance."

Corporations must to pivot toward human-centered strategies because building trust with workers is not just good ethics; it's good business.

CHAPTER 13

FUTUREPROOF YOUR GAME

"Level Up, Don't Become An 'Obsolete'."
– Mike Johns

In compiling this resource guide for "Death of a Job" readers, I've curated a diverse selection of AI workforce development opportunities to help you stay competitive in the rapidly evolving job market. This list of 20 recommended training courses and workshops spans free and paid options, catering to various skill levels and professional backgrounds.

The selection process prioritized:

1. Relevance: Courses that address current AI trends and workforce needs.
2. Credibility: Programs offered by reputable institutions and industry leaders.
3. Accessibility: A mix of free and paid options to suit different budgets.
4. Practical application: Training that provides hands-on experience and real-world skills.
5. Diversity: Courses covering various aspects of AI, from technical skills to strategic implementation.

Key highlights include:

- Free courses from tech giants like Google, Microsoft, and IBM, offering foundational AI knowledge.
- Specialized programs from academic institutions like Harvard, MIT, and Stanford for in-depth learning.
- Industry-specific courses, such as AI in education and supply chain management.
- Professional certifications for those looking to demonstrate their AI expertise.

This guide aims to empower you with the tools and knowledge needed to navigate the AI-driven workplace transformation. Whether you're looking to upskill, reskill, or gain a competitive edge, these resources provide a starting point for your AI learning journey.

Free Courses:

- **Google AI Courses** - Comprehensive introduction to AI fundamentals
- **Microsoft AI Course** - Covers basics through neural networks and deep learning
- **Harvard's "Introduction to AI with Python"** - 7-week course on AI concepts and algorithms
- **IBM's "Introduction to Artificial Intelligence"** - 13-hour course on AI basics and applications
- **AWS "Generative AI With Large Language Models"** - 16-hour course on LLMs and generative AI
- **Google AI Essentials** - 10-hour self-paced study on AI tools and responsible use
- **"AI for Early Childhood Education" by The Case HQ**
- **"Innovative Teaching with AI" by The Case HQ**
- **LinkedIn's AI course library** - 250 courses covering various AI topics
- **"Explore Text-to-Speech Using Generative AI" by IBM SkillsBuild**

Paid Courses:

- Certified AI Transformation Leader (CAITL™) by USAII® - 8-14 week program for business leaders
- Post Graduate Program in AI And Machine Learning by Caltech University - 12-month comprehensive program
- "AI in Education: Leveraging ChatGPT for Teaching" by Wharton University - 3-week course
- Stanford University's Artificial Intelligence Graduate Certificate - In-depth program on AI foundations
- MIT's Professional Certificate Program in Machine Learning and Artificial Intelligence - 16-day intensive course
- Info-Tech's AI Workforce Development Program - 12-week program for IT leaders and practitioners
- "Certified AI Business Strategist (CAIBS)" by The Case HQ
- "Certified AI Operations Manager" by The Case HQ
- "Certified AI Strategic HR Leader (AI SHRL)" by The Case HQ
- "Certified AI Supply Chain Specialist (AI SCS)" by The Case HQ

Remember, the AI landscape is constantly evolving. Stay curious, keep learning, and leverage these resources to future-proof your career in the age of artificial intelligence.

CHAPTER 14

RETHINKING EDUCATION IN THE AGE OF JOB DISPLACEMENT

"Education isn't just schools—it's communities rewriting the rules of opportunity."
– **Dr. Bosun Tijani,** Nigerian Minister of Communications

The rapid advancement of automation and artificial intelligence (AI) is fundamentally reshaping the American workforce, necessitating a radical transformation in our approach to education. The traditional educational model, rooted in agricultural-era schedules and industrial-era structures, is no longer sufficient to prepare students for the dynamic and technology-driven future they face.

The Current State of Education in America

While education policy has historically been decentralized, recent years have seen significant disparities emerge between states in terms of educational performance and outcomes. As of 2025, the top-performing states for public education are:

1. Massachusetts
2. New York
3. Connecticut
4. New Jersey
5. Virginia

These states have consistently invested in education, with high per-student expenditures, competitive teacher salaries, and strong academic outcomes. According to the 2024 *Consumer Affairs Report*, Massachusetts boasts a 96.1% high school graduation rate and the highest average ACT scores in the nation.

However, this success is not uniform across the country. Many states, particularly in the South and parts of the Midwest, lag significantly behind in educational outcomes and investment. This growing disparity threatens to exacerbate existing economic and social inequalities, potentially creating a two-tiered workforce ill-equipped to face the challenges of automation and AI.

The Imperative for Change

The need for a skills-based education system has never been more critical. By 2025, it's estimated that AI and automation will displace 85 million jobs globally while creating 97 million new ones. These new roles will require a different set of skills than those emphasized in traditional education.

Agentic AI in Education

Agentic AI, or AI systems that can act autonomously to achieve specific goals, has the potential to revolutionize education. These systems can:

- Provide personalized learning experiences tailored to each student's needs and pace.
- Offer real-time feedback and assessment, allowing for continuous improvement.

- Act as AI teaching assistants, handling routine tasks and freeing up human teachers for more complex interactions.

Accelerated Learning Through AI

Recent studies have shown the potential for AI to dramatically accelerate the learning process. For example, according to the "Impact Lab", a pilot program in Edo State, Nigeria, demonstrated that students using AI-assisted learning achieved the equivalent of two academic years of progress in just six weeks, a 1200% improvement. This acceleration is achieved through:

- Personalized curriculum adaptation
- Real-time progress tracking and adjustment
- Immersive, interactive learning experiences

International Models for AI in Education

Several countries are already implementing ambitious AI education programs that the United States could learn from:

- Lithuania's "Experience AI" program aims to teach 40,000 young people about artificial intelligence, focusing on practical skills and ethical considerations.
- South Korea has integrated AI into its classrooms, with teachers leading an AI revolution. This includes using AI for personalized learning, automated grading, and even AI-generated lesson plans.

The Path Forward for American Education

To prepare for the future of work and mitigate job displacement, the American education system must:

1. Shift focus from rote memorization to skills development, emphasizing critical thinking, creativity, and adaptability.
2. Integrate AI and technology into all aspects of education, from curriculum design to classroom management.

3. Implement continuous, lifelong learning models that allow workers to upskill and reskill throughout their careers.
4. Address state-level disparities through federal initiatives and increased funding for underperforming regions.
5. Partner with industry leaders to ensure curriculum relevance and provide real-world learning opportunities.

America Must Adapt or Leave Millions Behind

The transformation of the American education system is not just desirable; it's imperative for the nation's economic future and global competitiveness. By embracing AI, focusing on skills development, and learning from international best practices, the U.S. can create an education system that prepares all students for the challenges and opportunities of the AI-driven economy.

As we stand at this critical juncture, the choice is clear: adapt our educational approach to meet the demands of the future, or risk leaving millions of Americans behind in an increasingly automated world. The time for action is now.

Why Communities Must Lead

As AI reshapes labor markets, communities must lead the charge to prevent systemic inequities. Schools alone cannot close the AI skills gap—grassroots organizations like the Urban League, Boys & Girls Clubs of America, and community colleges are critical hubs for democratizing access to AI literacy. Without hyperlocal solutions, disparities will deepen: McKinsey projects that 40% of Black and Latino workers will face high displacement risk by 2030 due to automation.

1. **Equity Imperative:**
    - Rural and urban underserved districts lack AI infrastructure (e.g., Mississippi schools score 41/100 on digital readiness vs. Massachusetts' 92/100).

   - Local orgs understand cultural barriers: 68% of low-income families trust community centers over schools for tech training.
2. **AI as a Social Justice Tool:**
   - Example: Nigeria's Inspire Platform reduced youth unemployment 5% by aligning curricula with labor needs via community feedback.
3. **Sustainable Coexistence:**
   - EmergingRule's principle of "human-machine-nature harmony" demands place-based solutions (e.g., training farmers in AI-driven climate adaptation).

How Communities Can Lead: Action Plan

1. **Urban League Model: AI Justice Coalitions**
   - **AI Career Accelerators:** Partner with tech firms to offer:
     - Free prompt engineering bootcamps for displaced workers.
     - Algorithmic bias workshops to audit hiring AI tools used locally.
   - **Mobile AI Labs:** Deploy vans with VR/AI tutors to housing projects, replicating Nigeria's Learning Passport success.
2. **Boys & Girls Clubs: After-School AI Hubs**
   - **AI Creativity Zones:**
     - Teach youth to build chatbots addressing local issues (e.g., food insecurity mapping).
     - Use tools like Agentic AI Tutors to compress skill gaps (see Edo State's 62% score gains in 6 weeks).
   - **Parent Upskilling:** Host "AI 101" nights to bridge generational digital divides.
3. **Community Colleges: Reskilling Engines**
   - **Micro-Credential Partnerships:**
     - Offer 8-week certifications in AI auditing, data labeling, and robotics maintenance.

- Example: Miami Dade College's "AI for Healthcare" program placed 92% of graduates in jobs.
- **AI Mentorship Networks:** Pair students with local tech professionals for project-based learning.

Policy Levers for Community Success

Federal-Community AI Grants:

- Fund "AI Equity Zones" prioritizing ZIP codes with <50% broadband access.

Algorithmic Transparency Mandates:

- Require EdTech companies to share training data sources with community review boards.

Tax Incentives:

- Offer businesses credits for sponsoring AI labs at community centers.

Case Study: Detroit's Community-Led AI Revival

- **Challenge:** 32% adult AI illiteracy, auto industry job losses.
- **Solution:**
  - Henry Ford College + Urban League launched free "AI Manufacturing Certificates".
  - Boys & Girls Clubs integrated AI tutors into STEM programs, boosting graduation rates 18%.
- **Result:** 4,000+ workers reskilled; $50M in new tech investments.

Call to Action: Build Hyperlocal AI Ecosystems

Steps for Immediate Impact:

1. **Map Assets:** Partner with libraries, churches, and rec centers to host AI labs.

2. **Train Community AI Ambassadors:** Recruit 100 locals per city for AI literacy train-the-trainer programs.
3. **Demand Equitable Tools:** Advocate for open-source AI platforms (e.g., Nigeria's IGNITE) to avoid corporate lock-in.

The Cost of Waiting

Without community-led AI education:

- 9.2M U.S. workers could face permanent unemployment by 2030.
- Rural-urban wage gaps may widen by 37% due to AI skill disparities.

Why Communities Must Lead

As AI reshapes labor markets, communities must lead the charge to prevent systemic inequities. Schools alone cannot close the AI skills gap—grassroots organizations like the Urban League, Boys & Girls Clubs of America, and community colleges are critical hubs for democratizing access to AI literacy. Without hyperlocal solutions, disparities will deepen: McKinsey projects 40% of Black and Latino workers face high displacement risk by 2030 due to automation.

Building Hyperlocal Pathways to AI Equity

The AI revolution demands more than top-down policy solutions—it requires grassroots coalitions of trusted institutions working in concert. Organizations like Harlem's Uptown Neighborhood Initiatives & Logistics (funded by the Center for Justice Innovation) exemplify this approach, blending vocational training, AI literacy programs, and employer partnerships to create pipelines from poverty to prosperity. As displacement accelerates, these hyperlocal networks will become society's first responders in the fight for equitable AI readiness.

Why Local Institutions Matter Most

- **Trusted Access Points:** Public libraries, community colleges, and Boys & Girls Clubs serve as lifelines for marginalized learners. Example: Harlem's Employment and Technology Center combines VR training with culinary arts, proving STEM education can honor cultural assets.
- **Bridging the Last Mile:** Programs like UMEZ's Hospitality Bridge Training and MEOC's nurse aide certifications align curricula with immediate job openings, while App-In Club models prepare youth for emerging AI roles.
- **Corporate-Community Synergy:** NVIDIA's AI Pathways partnership with Boys & Girls Clubs shows how tech firms can equip local hubs with tools like Jetbot robotics kits—scaling access without sacrificing community oversight.

Blueprint for the Next Decade

1. **AI Pop-Up Hubs:** Deploy mobile labs (modeled on Best Buy Teen Tech Centers) to libraries and Starbucks meetups, offering:
   - Free prompt engineering workshops using MIT App Inventor
   - "AI Career Clinics" where community college students coach residents on resumé-building with ChatGPT
2. **Justice-Centered Upskilling:**
   - Train outreach workers as AI Navigators through programs like HCCI's digital literacy initiatives, focusing on auditing hiring algorithms for bias.
   - Expand the Urban League's apprenticeship models to include AI auditing roles in healthcare and construction sectors.
3. **Policy Meets Pavement:**

- Mandate that 20% of corporate AI R&D budgets fund community lab partnerships (e.g., Harlem's VR architecture programs).
- Reward employers who hire from local upskilling pipelines with tax breaks tied to retention metrics.

The Stakes:

Without these networks, McKinsey's projected 40% displacement risk for Black and Latino workers by 2030 will become reality. But models like Uptown Neighborhood Initiatives prove alternatives exist—their blended approach reduced youth unemployment 18% by connecting AI training to hospitality jobs at the Marriott Renaissance.

"The future belongs to cities that turn bodegas into coding hubs and libraries into AI dojos."

One thing I know: equitable AI adoption won't be led by Silicon Valley, but by coalitions of community colleges, nonprofits, and corner cafes—where trust is earned, not algorithmically generated. The blueprint exists; now we must scale it block by block.

CHAPTER 15

BECOME A LIFETIME STUDENT

"If I were a student today, I would learn how to use AI tools like ChatGPT, Gemini Pro, and Grok. These skills are essential for staying relevant in an increasingly AI-driven world."
– **Jensen Huang,** CEO of Nvidia

Lifelong Learning: Staying Relevant in the AI Economy

In the new economy shaped by artificial intelligence, education can no longer be a one-time achievement ending with a degree. Lifelong learning has become essential for individuals to adapt, upskill, and reskill continually in order to remain competitive in an AI-dominated world. This shift reflects the rapid pace of technological advancement, where jobs evolve or disappear while entirely new roles emerge. The ability to learn continuously is now a survival skill, not merely an option.

Platforms and Resources for Lifelong Learning

Accessible platforms like **YouTube** have democratized education, offering free resources on generative AI and advanced topics. Channels such as **Google Cloud Tech** and **iN-**

euron Intelligence provide tutorials that empower learners to dive into AI concepts at their own pace. For those seeking structured programs, **community colleges** are stepping up as key players in this transformation. These institutions offer affordable certificates and associate degrees tailored to regional workforce needs, often developed in collaboration with local industries.

AI-driven tools like **Degreed**, **LinkedIn Learning**, and **SkillLab** further enhance the learning process by personalizing training paths based on individual skill gaps and career goals. These platforms track progress in real time, helping workers stay agile and competitive in fields like technology, healthcare, and manufacturing.

AI Personas in the Workforce

As AI reshapes employment landscapes, workers exhibit diverse attitudes toward its adoption. Slack's research identifies five distinct personas that define how individuals approach AI integration:

1. **Innovators (Bloomers)**: Enthusiastically embrace AI and collaborate on responsible solutions.
2. **Cautionaries (Gloomers)**: Advocate for stricter regulations to ensure ethical use of AI.
3. **Accelerators (Zoomers)**: Push for rapid implementation with minimal restrictions due to its benefits.
4. **Resistors (Doomers)**: Oppose AI outright, focusing solely on its risks and negative impacts.
5. **Adaptors**: Pragmatically adjust to AI integration without strong enthusiasm or resistance.

Understanding these personas is crucial for employers and educators as they develop strategies to onboard workers into "The AI Team"—a workplace where humans and AI collaborate effectively.

Why Lifelong Learning Matters

The rise of AI is not just about automation; it's about transformation—creating opportunities for innovation while simultaneously disrupting traditional roles. Studies predict that while AI may displace millions of jobs globally, it will also generate 97 million new roles by 2025 in areas like machine learning, data analysis, and digital marketing. Lifelong learning ensures individuals can pivot into these emerging fields rather than being left behind.

Moreover, lifelong learning fosters adaptability—a critical skill in a world where staying still means falling behind. It empowers individuals to navigate interdisciplinary opportunities, such as combining expertise in agriculture with AI-driven analytics or leveraging fintech knowledge alongside machine learning tools.

How Communities Can Support Lifelong Learning

Local outreach organizations are uniquely positioned to play a pivotal role in fostering lifelong learning by providing accessible resources and personalized support:

- **Harlem's Uptown Neighborhood Initiatives & Logistics**, funded by the Center for Justice Innovation, offers vocational training programs that align with community needs while integrating cutting-edge technologies like VR for hands-on learning.
- **Urban League** chapters provide free workshops on AI literacy and job readiness tailored to underserved populations.
- **Boys & Girls Clubs of America** have begun incorporating STEM-focused after-school programs powered by generative AI tools.
- **Best Buy Teen Centers** offer tech labs where youth can explore robotics and coding through interactive projects.
- **Community colleges**, public libraries, and even informal meetups at local Starbucks are evolving into

hubs for lifelong learning—providing spaces where individuals can network, access resources, and collaborate on projects that prepare them for the future.

These organizations bridge gaps left by traditional educational systems by making learning accessible to all demographics—especially vulnerable groups like immigrants or adults with basic skills gaps—through tailored programs powered by AI tools such as Babbel, Duolingo, or Jobiri.

Lifelong Learning as a Collective Responsibility

Lifelong learning is no longer optional; it is the cornerstone of success in an AI-driven economy. Platforms like YouTube, community colleges, and AI-powered tools have made continuous education more accessible than ever before. However, local outreach organizations such as Harlem's Uptown Neighborhood Initiatives & Logistics, Urban League chapters, Boys & Girls Clubs of America, Best Buy Teen Centers, public libraries, and informal community meetups are critical for ensuring equitable access to these opportunities.

By embracing lifelong learning as a shared responsibility—between individuals, communities, institutions, and governments—we can transform disruption into empowerment. Together, we can build ecosystems where every person has the chance to thrive amidst technological change. In this new era of education, adaptability is not just a skill—it's the key to unlocking human potential in the age of automation.

CHAPTER 16

COMPARISON OF JOB SKILLS IN 2025 VS. 2030

"Artificial intelligence, deep learning, machine learning—whatever you're doing, if you don't understand it—learn it. Because otherwise, you're going to be a dinosaur within three years."
– **Mark Cuban,** Entrepreneur and Investor

By 2030, job skills will reflect a greater emphasis on advanced technical expertise (e.g., AI, big data) paired with human-centric abilities such as creative thinking, empathy, and systems thinking. This evolution highlights the growing complexity of the global workforce as it adapts to technological advancements, environmental challenges, and demographic shifts. Lifelong learning will no longer be optional—it will be essential for workers to remain relevant in an ever-changing job market. Here are **10 key differences** in job skills required in 2025 versus those anticipated for 2030, based on evolving trends in technology, societal needs, and workforce demands:

1. Technological Literacy

- **2025:** Basic technological literacy (e.g., proficiency with digital tools) is essential for most roles.
- **2030:** Advanced skills in AI, big data, networks, and cybersecurity become critical as technology integration deepens.

2. Creative Thinking

- **2025:** Creative thinking is valued but secondary to technical skills.
- **2030:** It becomes a core skill, driving innovation in green technologies, AI applications, and digital transformation.

3. Resilience and Flexibility

- **2025:** Workers need resilience to adapt to pandemic-driven disruptions and economic uncertainty.
- **2030:** Flexibility becomes vital for navigating rapid industry shifts caused by automation, climate adaptation, and demographic changes.

4. Leadership and Social Influence

- **2025:** Leadership focuses on managing teams effectively within organizations.
- **2030:** Leadership evolves to include influencing societal change, particularly in sustainability and diversity initiatives.

5. Curiosity and Lifelong Learning

- **2025:** Lifelong learning is encouraged but not universally practiced.
- **2030:** It becomes mandatory as nearly 39% of current skills will transform or become obsolete by this time.

6. Environmental Stewardship

- **2025:** Limited emphasis on green economy-related skills.
- **2030:** Skills like environmental engineering, renewable energy systems, and carbon reduction strategies are in high demand due to the green transition.

7. Problem-Solving Complexity

- **2025:** Problem-solving focuses on critical thinking for structured challenges.
- **2030:** Systems thinking emerges as a necessity for addressing complex global issues like climate change and resource management.

8. Empathy and Active Listening

- **2025:** Emotional intelligence is valued primarily for team collaboration and customer service roles.
- **2030:** It becomes central to talent management and mentoring as aging economies demand stronger interpersonal skills for workforce development.

9. Talent Management

- **2025:** Managing talent is important for organizational efficiency and team performance.
- **2030:** Talent management expands to include motivating diverse teams amid demographic shifts and fostering inclusive workplaces.

10. AI Integration

- **2025:** Workers adapt to AI tools assisting tasks like data analysis or customer service automation.
- **2030:** Workers must collaborate seamlessly with AI systems while leveraging human creativity and ethical judgment to complement machine capabilities.

The Evolution of Job Skills

The comparison of job skills required in 2025 versus those anticipated for 2030 underscores the profound transformation of the workforce driven by technological advancements, global challenges, and shifting societal priorities. By 2030, the nature of work will demand not only technical expertise but also human-centric abilities that machines cannot replicate—creativity, empathy, systems thinking, and adaptability. Workers will need to continuously evolve their skillsets to remain relevant, as nearly 39% of current skills are expected to become obsolete or require transformation.

This matters because the future of work is not just about automation replacing jobs—it's about creating opportunities for innovation and collaboration between humans and AI. The rise of systems thinking and environmental stewardship reflects a growing need for solutions to interconnected global issues like climate change and resource management. Similarly, the increasing emphasis on creative thinking and emotional intelligence highlights the importance of uniquely human capabilities in driving progress.

The Role of Communities in Skill Development

Local organizations will play a critical role in preparing individuals for this shift. Programs like Harlem's Uptown Neighborhood Initiatives & Logistics, funded by the Center for Justice Innovation, demonstrate how outreach efforts can upskill communities and align training with emerging industries. Institutions such as **Urban League**, **Boys & Girls Clubs of America**, **Best Buy Teen Centers**, **community colleges**, **public libraries**, and even informal meetups at Starbucks are uniquely positioned to act as hubs for lifelong learning. These organizations can:

- Provide accessible training in AI-related fields like data analysis, cybersecurity, and environmental engineering.
- Foster collaboration between local industries and educational programs to ensure alignment with labor market demands.
- Bridge digital divides by offering resources such as broadband access, AI literacy programs, and mentorship opportunities.

A Call to Action

The evolution from 2025 to 2030 is not merely a timeline—it's a roadmap for redefining education and workforce development. Governments must prioritize funding for reskilling initiatives, while employers should invest in programs that prepare workers to collaborate with AI systems rather than be replaced by them. Communities must embrace their role as catalysts for change, ensuring equitable access to resources that empower individuals to thrive in an AI-driven economy.

Ultimately, the future belongs to those who adapt—those who embrace lifelong learning as a way of life rather than a one-time endeavor. By fostering ecosystems where creativity meets technology and resilience meets opportunity, we can transform the challenges ahead into a legacy of progress and empowerment for generations to come. The evolution of job skills is not just about survival; it's about unlocking human potential in ways we've yet to imagine.

CHAPTER 17

JOBS THAT WILL COME AND GO BY 2030

"Be Afraid. Be Extremely Afraid... Because You Could Be Next... Let The Revolution Begin..."
– Noah Kross, *The Humanity Bureau*

20 Job Titles Likely to Become Obsolete by 2030 and Their Impact on Demographics

Here are **20 job titles** expected to face significant automation or elimination by 2030 due to advancements in AI and robotics. The analysis also highlights which demographic groups will suffer the most based on overrepresentation in these roles.

Jobs Likely to Become Obsolete

1. Data Entry Clerks

- **Why:** AI-powered systems can process vast amounts of data faster and more accurately.
- **Impact:** Women and Black workers, who are overrepresented in administrative roles, will be disproportionately affected.

2. Telemarketers

- **Why:** Automated sales calls and chatbots are replacing human telemarketers.
- **Impact:** Mexican and Black workers, often employed in call centers, will face higher job losses.

3. Fast Food Workers

- **Why:** Robots and kiosks are increasingly handling food preparation and cashier tasks.
- **Impact:** Black and Hispanic workers, heavily employed in the fast-food industry, will be hit hardest.

4. Manufacturing Assemblers

- **Why:** Industrial robots are taking over repetitive assembly tasks.
- **Impact:** Asian and Mexican workers, who dominate manufacturing roles, will see significant displacement.

5. Cashiers

- **Why:** Contactless payment systems and cashier-less stores like Amazon Go reduce the need for human cashiers.
- **Impact:** Women, particularly Black and Hispanic women, will experience higher unemployment.

6. Travel Agents

- **Why:** Online booking platforms have made travel agencies largely redundant.
- **Impact:** Women, who historically dominate this field, will be disproportionately affected.

7. Customer Service Representatives

- **Why:** AI chatbots handle routine inquiries more efficiently than humans.

- **Impact:** Black workers, who are overrepresented in customer service roles, will face significant losses.

8. Bookkeepers and Accountants

- **Why:** Automated accounting software eliminates manual bookkeeping tasks.
- **Impact:** Women, who dominate accounting roles, will face challenges transitioning to new fields.

9. Proofreaders and Translators

- **Why:** Natural Language Processing (NLP) tools like ChatGPT automate basic proofreading and translation tasks.
- **Impact:** Asian workers may experience job losses due to their representation in translation services.

10. Radiologists and Diagnostic Technicians

- **Why:** AI systems can analyze medical images with high accuracy, reducing reliance on human radiologists.
- **Impact:** Women in healthcare roles may face displacement as diagnostic tasks become automated.

11. Financial Analysts

- **Why:** AI tools can perform routine financial analysis faster than humans.
- **Impact:** Black workers transitioning into higher-paying financial roles may lose opportunities due to automation.

12. Administrative Assistants

- **Why:** Virtual assistants powered by AI handle scheduling and organizational tasks efficiently.
- **Impact:** Women, especially Black women in office support roles, will face higher displacement rates.

13. Retail Salespeople

- **Why:** E-commerce platforms and AI recommendation systems reduce the need for physical retail staff.
- **Impact:** Hispanic workers employed in retail will bear the brunt of these changes.

14. Taxi Drivers/Uber Drivers

- **Why:** Autonomous vehicles are replacing human drivers for ride-sharing services.
- **Impact:** Mexican workers heavily employed in transportation roles will suffer significant losses.

15. Letter Carriers

- **Why:** Digital communication has reduced demand for traditional mail delivery services.
- **Impact:** Other minorities working as postal employees may face job cuts

16. Fast Food Delivery Drivers

- **Why:** Drone delivery systems are replacing human drivers for food delivery services.
- **Impact:** Mexican workers employed in delivery services will be disproportionately impacted.

17. Content Writers for Basic Tasks

- **Why:** AI tools like Jasper automate mundane writing tasks such as product descriptions or reports.
- **Impact:** Women employed in entry-level content creation roles may lose opportunities.

18. Market Research Analysts

- **Why:** AI can analyze vast datasets more efficiently than humans for market trends and insights.

- **Impact:** Asian workers employed in analytical roles may see job reductions.

19. Mechanics (Basic Repairs)

- **Why:** Automated diagnostic tools reduce the need for manual mechanical repairs in vehicles or appliances.
- **Impact:** Black men without college degrees working in production repair roles will be disproportionately affected.

20. Secretaries/Office Support Staff

- **Why:** AI tools streamline scheduling, communication, and document management tasks traditionally handled by secretaries.
- **Impact:** Women, particularly Black women, will experience higher rates of displacement due to automation.

Job Loss by 2030 by Demographic Group

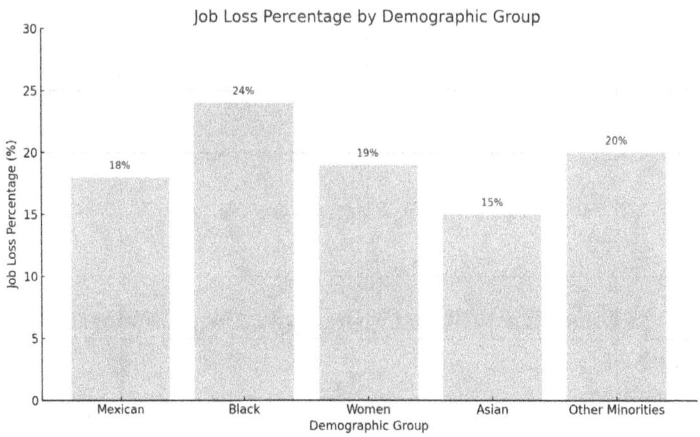

(Data Source: LinkedIn)

This data highlights how automation disproportionately impacts marginalized groups like Black workers (24%) and women (19%), exacerbating existing inequalities.

Addressing Inequities Through Reskilling

The automation-driven obsolescence of jobs underscores the urgent need for equitable reskilling initiatives targeting vulnerable demographics such as Black workers, women, and Hispanic communities disproportionately affected by these

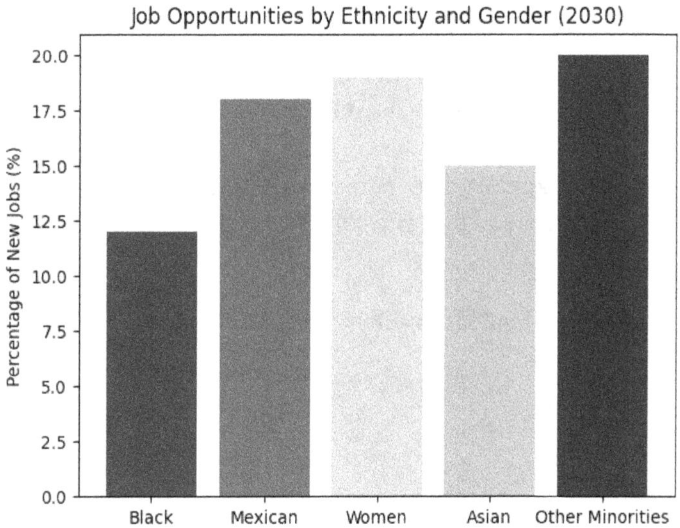

Job Opportunities by Ethnicity and Gender (2030)

25 Jobs That Will Be Created by 2030: A Demographic Analysis

Based on emerging trends in technology, sustainability, and societal needs, here are **25 new or rapidly growing jobs** expected to be prominent by 2030, alongside an analysis of how different ethnic and gender groups are positioned to access these opportunities.

Technology and AI-Driven Roles

1. **AI Ethics Officer:** Ensures ethical use of AI systems. Asian and White workers currently hold a stronger position in this area due to existing representation in tech, with Black and Mexican workers needing increased access.
2. **Algorithm Bias Auditor:** Evaluates and corrects biases in AI algorithms. Asians are slightly better-positioned.
3. **Autonomous Vehicle Specialist:** Manages self-driving vehicles. White and Asian men have advantages due to current educational trends.
4. **Internet of Things (IoT) Specialist:** Designs interconnected smart devices. Asian men currently have a strong presence in hardware.
5. **Quantum Computing Developer:** Builds quantum computing applications. Asians are in prime position.
6. **Cybersecurity Resilience Analyst:** Protects systems from cyber threats. Current industry is diverse with growing demand.
7. **Augmented Reality (AR) Journey Builder:** Creates immersive AR experiences. This will demand skill so the race is yet to be determined.
8. **Metaverse Planner:** Develops virtual environments. White and Asian workers in tech are well positioned.
9. **Digital Twin Engineer:** Designs virtual replicas of physical systems. White and Asian workers in tech are well positioned.
10. **Human-Machine Interaction Designer:** Enhances collaboration between humans and AI/robots. A diverse field so this race is up for grab

Sustainability and Green Economy Roles

11. **Renewable Energy Technician:** Installs renewable energy systems. High opportunity field for workers of all backgrounds.

12. **Carbon Reduction Strategist:** Develops carbon footprint reduction plans. Strong chance for White and Asian individuals.
13. **Rewilder:** Restores natural ecosystems. This is a race for all.
14. **Climate Adaptation Specialist:** Designs infrastructure for climate change. Race is still up for grabs.
15. **Biofilm Installer:** Installs sustainable building materials. Race is still up for grabs.

Healthcare and Biotechnology Roles

16. **Organ Creator:** Engineers transplantable organs. White and Asian men are well-positioned due to existing educational trends.
17. **Genomic Data Analyst:** Interprets genetic data. Asians will most likely dominate.
18. **Neurotechnology Specialist:** Develops brain-computer interfaces. Asians will dominate

Education and Training Roles

19. **AI Trainer/Educator:** Teaches individuals to work with AI systems. Strong opportunity for Black and Mexican workers with targeted training.
20. **Virtual Learning Environment Designer:** Builds immersive online education platforms.

Infrastructure and Urban Development Roles

21. **Makeshift Structure Engineer:** Designs temporary housing solutions. The race is still up for grabs.
22. **Smart City Planner:** Develops urban areas with smart technologies. Race is still up for grabs.

Creative and Cultural Roles

23. **Experience Designer for Virtual Worlds:** Creates interactive content for gaming. Mostly women and people of color lead this area.

Other Emerging Roles

24. **Space Tourism Guide/Planner:** Organizes space travel experiences. White dominate.
25. **Drone Traffic Controller:** Manages airspace for drones. The race is still up for grabs.

CHAPTER 18

A CALL TO ACTION FOR COLLEGE STUDENTS AND YOUNG ENTREPRENEURS

"We must invest in education that empowers all students to shape the future of AI."
– **Fei-Fei Li,** Co-Director, Stanford Human-Centered AI Institute

The Right Time: Young Adults Strategy

For those of you aged 18 to 25, you've been handed the opportunity of a lifetime. This moment in history is your chance to shape the future, much like the pioneers of the personal computer (PC) revolution did decades ago.

The Power of Timing

Take Steve Jobs as an example. His success wasn't just because he was brilliant—it was also because he was born at precisely the right time. Jobs, born in 1955, was a 21-year-old college dropout when he and Steve Wozniak started Apple in a garage. They were perfectly positioned to ride the wave of the PC revolution. If Jobs had been born ten years earlier or later, Apple might never have existed.

Jobs wasn't alone. His generation included visionaries like Bill Gates (born 1955), Larry Ellison (born 1944), and Michael Dell (born 1965). These innovators caught the same wave, and their companies—Apple, Microsoft, Oracle, and Dell—dominated because they were young, hungry, and ready at the exact moment personal computing exploded onto the scene.

Their brilliance mattered, but timing was everything. And now, we're at a similar inflection point with artificial intelligence (AI). Just as they seized their moment during the PC revolution, this is your moment to lead during the AI revolution.

Seeing Opportunity in Uncertainty

While others may see uncertainty in today's rapidly changing world, you should see possibility. You have the chance to become the architects of humanity's next chapter. But to seize this opportunity, you need to avoid falling into outdated traps—especially those tied to traditional education.

The Trap of Traditional Education

Traditional education was designed for a world that's disappearing. Spending four to seven years specializing in one narrow field is now one of the riskiest moves you can make as a young person. The pace of change is so fast that no career path feels guaranteed anymore.

Instead of locking yourself into a rigid framework, position yourself at the center of this revolution by mastering AI-related skills. Learn how to build and manage AI agents. Whether through coding or no-code platforms, there are countless tools and resources available online that can help you get started.

How to Get Started

1. **Learn AI Automation Skills:**
   - If you're interested in coding, it only takes a few months to learn basic programming skills like Python or JavaScript.
   - Alternatively, explore no-code platforms that allow you to create AI solutions without needing extensive technical knowledge.
2. **Leverage Online Resources:**
   - Traditional colleges won't have courses tailored for this fast-moving field yet. Instead, roll up your sleeves and seek out free or affordable online courses.
   - Communities and platforms dedicated to AI learning can provide invaluable support and guidance.
3. **Take Action Quickly:**
   - The world of AI evolves rapidly; staying ahead means being proactive about learning and experimenting with new tools.

Two Career Paths with AI Skills

Once you've built a foundation in AI automation skills, there are two primary paths you can take:

1. *Join-A-Company:*
   Every company will soon need AI automation specialists. With these skills, you can secure high-paying roles helping businesses integrate AI into their operations.
2. *Start-Your-Own-Agency:*
   If you're entrepreneurial, consider starting an AI automation agency. You can work with businesses to help them transition into the AI era by building custom solutions or managing their automation needs.

Your Moment is Now

This is your time—your version of the PC revolution—but for AI. By developing the right skills and embracing this transformative era, you can position yourself as a leader in shaping humanity's next chapter. Don't wait for permission or rely on outdated systems; take charge of your future today.

"AI may be the engine of the future, but wisdom acts as its navigator, guiding our course through the vast, uncharted waters of technology and society."
– Source: AI itself

CHAPTER 19

FROM OG TO AI EXPERT: TURNING EXPERIENCE INTO AI EXPERTISE

"Age is an asset in the AI era."
– Mike Johns

In a world increasingly driven by artificial intelligence (AI), many individuals over 45 fear they may be "too old" to adapt or contribute meaningfully. This fear is rooted in the misconception that innovation and technological progress are the domains of the young. However, history and research tell a different story. Far from being a liability, age brings with it unique advantages—real-world experience, practical wisdom, and the ability to apply insights that younger generations may lack. These qualities are not only relevant but critical in shaping the future of AI.

The Evidence: Great Innovations Come Later in Life

A study by the National Bureau of Economic Research (NBER) challenges the conventional wisdom that innovation peaks in youth. His research shows that over the past century, the average age at which individuals produce notable inventions has steadily increased. For example:

Age Distribution of Innovators:

- 42% of innovations were made by individuals in their 30s.
- 40% occurred in their 40s.
- A significant 14% came from those over 50.

This data underscores that groundbreaking achievements are not confined to youth but often emerge from decades of accumulated knowledge and experience.

Jones also found that the mean age of great achievement has risen by five to six years per century. This trend reflects the increasing importance of experience over raw ability, as well as longer life expectancies and extended periods of education and training. In essence, older innovators are thriving because their expertise allows them to navigate complex challenges more effectively than their younger counterparts.

Why Experience Matters in AI

As AI continues to evolve, it relies heavily on human input for training, decision-making frameworks, and ethical considerations. Here's why professionals aged 45+ bring unparalleled value:

1. **Practical Wisdom:**
   Decades of navigating real-world challenges equip older professionals with a nuanced understanding of industries, systems, and human behavior—qualities essential for designing AI systems that are both effective and ethical.
2. **Domain Expertise:**
   Many AI applications require deep knowledge of specific fields such as healthcare, finance, or manufacturing. Professionals with years of experience in these areas can guide AI development to ensure relevance and accuracy.
3. **Ethical Oversight:**
   The ethical implications of AI—bias in algorithms, data privacy concerns, and societal impact—demand

mature judgment and a long-term perspective. Older professionals are uniquely positioned to lead these discussions.

4. **Mentorship & Leadership:**
   The ability to mentor younger colleagues and lead cross-generational teams is invaluable in fostering collaboration between seasoned experts and tech-savvy newcomers.

Debunking the "Too Old" Myth

The myth of being "too old" for innovation stems from outdated stereotypes about aging and technology. However, history provides ample examples of late-stage success:

- **Steve Jobs' Renaissance:** Jobs was in his mid-40s when he returned to Apple and launched iconic products like the iPod and iPhone.
- **Nobel Prize Winners:** Many Nobel laureates achieve their most significant breakthroughs well into their 40s or later.
- **Modern AI Entrepreneurs:** Today's rapidly evolving AI landscape is creating opportunities for experienced professionals to leverage their insights in ways younger innovators cannot.

How to Thrive in the AI Era After 45

For those over 45 looking to remain relevant or pivot into AI-related roles, here's a roadmap:

1. **Leverage Your Experience:**
   Focus on areas where your expertise complements AI technologies—such as training machine learning models with industry-specific data or advising on ethical frameworks.
2. **Upskill Strategically:**
   Take advantage of online resources to learn about AI tools and platforms. No-code solutions make it easier

than ever for non-technical professionals to engage with AI.

3. **Collaborate Across Generations:**
   Partner with younger colleagues who bring technical skills while contributing your strategic vision and leadership.
4. **Embrace Lifelong Learning:**
   Stay curious and open to new ideas by continuously updating your knowledge base through courses, webinars, or professional networks.
5. **Position Yourself as a Thought Leader:**
   Share your insights through writing, speaking engagements, or consulting roles to establish yourself as an authority at the intersection of your field and AI.

Redefining Innovation Across Ages

The rise of AI does not signal the end of opportunity for older professionals; rather, it marks a new beginning where experience is more valuable than ever. As Benjamin Jones' research demonstrates, great inventions often come later in life. By embracing change, leveraging their unique strengths, and committing to lifelong learning, individuals aged 45+ can position themselves as indispensable contributors to the AI revolution.

The myth of being "too old" is just that—a myth. The reality is clear: innovation knows no age limit.

CHAPTER 20

CHINA VERSUS THE WORLD: A GOVERNMENT-LED REVOLUTION IN AI EDUCATION

"Continued American leadership in Artificial Intelligence is of paramount importance to maintaining the economic and national security of the United States."
– President Donald J. Trump

Starting September 1, 2025, China will implement a groundbreaking policy mandating AI education for all primary and secondary school students. Children as young as six will receive at least eight hours of annual instruction in artificial intelligence, covering topics ranging from basic concepts to advanced applications like machine learning and robotics as they progress through school. This initiative is not just an educational reform; it is a bold, centralized strategy designed to position China as the global leader in AI innovation.

Key Features of China's Strategy:

- **Nationwide Mandate:** AI education is now as fundamental as reading and math, ensuring universal access across all regions.
- **Early Exposure:** Age-appropriate activities introduce young children to AI concepts, fostering curiosity and foundational skills.
- **Integration with Industry:** Partnerships between schools and tech giants like Huawei and Alibaba align education with workforce demands.
- **University Pipeline:** Over 345 universities offer AI majors, supported by 34 dedicated AI institutes, creating a seamless transition from K-12 to higher education.

This centralized approach ensures that every citizen is equipped with the skills necessary for an AI-driven economy. By embedding AI literacy into the national curriculum, China aims to cultivate a generation of creators and innovators who will drive breakthroughs in emerging technologies like quantum computing and autonomous systems.

America's Decentralized Approach: Fragmented Progress

In contrast, the United States lacks a cohesive national strategy for AI education. AI literacy initiatives are largely left to state governments and private organizations, resulting in significant disparities in access and quality. While some states, like California and Mississippi, have made strides in integrating AI into their curricula, these efforts remain isolated and inconsistent.

Challenges in the U.S. Model:

- **No Federal Mandate:** Unlike China, there is no nationwide requirement for AI education; states independently decide whether to adopt such programs.

- **Unequal Access:** According to the Center on Reinventing Public Education (CRPE) Rural and high-poverty districts lag behind suburban schools in adopting AI tools due to limited resources.
- **Industry Reliance:** Private-sector initiatives like Google's "AI for Everyone" fill gaps but lack coordination with public education systems.
- **Teacher Training Deficit:** Only 18% of U.S. K-12 teachers use AI tools in classrooms, with many reporting insufficient training. (CRPE).

While decentralization allows for experimentation and innovation, it exacerbates disparities in curriculum rigor and student outcomes. Without a unified strategy, America risks falling behind in the race for global AI leadership.

Long-Term Implications: What This Means for America

China's all-inclusive strategy will likely yield a generation of workers who are not only proficient in using AI but skilled in developing it. By 2030, artificial intelligence is expected to contribute nearly $20 trillion to the global economy, with countries leading in AI literacy poised to dominate economic growth and military advancements.

For America, the consequences of falling behind are severe:

- **Economic Vulnerability:** Automation driven by AI could eliminate 30% of U.S. jobs by 2030, particularly in manufacturing and logistics.
- **Talent Shortage:** China graduates twice as many STEM PhDs as the U.S., threatening America's ability to maintain its technological edge.
- **National Security Risks:** A lack of AI expertise could undermine U.S. defense capabilities against adversaries leveraging advanced technologies.

Solutions: What America Must Do Immediately

To compete with China's centralized model, the United States must adopt a more coordinated approach to AI education. Below are five actionable steps:

1. Federal Standards for AI Literacy

Mandate AI education nationwide by incorporating it into existing STEM curricula under the Every Student Succeeds Act (ESSA). Ensure all students learn foundational concepts like algorithms and ethical considerations starting in elementary school.

2. Teacher Training Revolution

Invest heavily in professional development programs for educators. Offer stipends for teachers who complete certifications in AI pedagogy, prioritizing underserved districts.

3. Democratize Access to Resources

Deploy high-performance computing resources to rural schools via federal grants. Create open-source platforms that provide free access to AI tools for educators and students.

4. Strengthen Industry Partnerships

Encourage tech companies like NVIDIA and Microsoft to fund K-12 AI labs through tax incentives. Establish public-private partnerships to align educational goals with workforce needs.

5. Expand STEM Immigration Policies

Fast-track visas for international students specializing in AI-related fields while increasing domestic investment in STEM programs at universities.

A New Space Race

China's mandatory AI education policy is not just about teaching children—it is about shaping the future of global power dynamics. For America, this moment mirrors the Sputnik challenge of 1957: complacency is not an option. To remain competitive, the U.S. must act decisively to create a unified strategy that democratizes access to AI education while fostering innovation across all levels of society.

The question is no longer whether America can compete—it's whether it will rise to meet this new frontier or fall behind as others shape the future.

CHAPTER 21

GLOBAL AI EDUCATION INITIATIVES: AMERICA'S POSITION IN THE NEW EDUCATIONAL ARMS RACE

"Democracy cannot succeed unless those who express their choice are prepared to choose wisely. The real safeguard of democracy, therefore, is education."
– **Franklin D. Roosevelt,** 32nd President of the United States

The race to integrate artificial intelligence into national education systems has emerged as a defining challenge of the 2020s, with countries worldwide implementing strategic initiatives to prepare their citizens for an AI-driven future. America's position in this landscape reveals concerning gaps compared to global competitors who have adopted more centralized, comprehensive approaches.

Global AI Education Landscape

Country	AI Education Approach
China	Nationwide mandatory AI education starting at age 6
Estonia	"AI Leap" program for all schools
Singapore	"World leader in AI by 2030" vision
South Korea	National-level AI curriculum
India	AI integrated into national curricula
United Arab Emirates	Strategic AI investments and smart governance
Canada	Local and civil society initiatives
United States	State-level initiatives, no federal mandate

Implementation Strategy	Current Status
Centralized Ministry oversight; 8+ annual hours of AI instruction	345 universities with AI majors; target of 500K AI professionals by 2025
National initiative launching September 1, 2025; inspired by historic "Tiger Leap" digital program	Public-private partnership providing free access to leading AI applications for all students
By 2026, AI training for teachers at all levels	AICET research center working with Ministry of Education on implementation
By 2025, AI coursework across all grade levels	Implementing personalized AI tutors for each student; adapting assignments based on learning behaviors
Using AI for student performance prediction and early intervention	Ranked 4th globally in AI according to Stanford's AI Index; ed-tech companies like Embibe using AI for math/science education
Heavy focus on higher education	University leaders show highest adoption of generative AI globally (54%)
No centralized mandate, but strong adoption	54% of college students use GenAI for studies; ranked 4th in Global AI Superpowers list
Fragmented implementation varying by state/district	Only 51% of high schools offer computer science; only 20% of college students use GenAI; 68% of educators report no AI training

America's Position: Decentralized and Falling Behind

While the United States remains the global leader in AI research and development (ranked #1 in Stanford's AI Index with a score of 70.06), its approach to AI education reveals significant challenges:

Fragmented Implementation: Unlike China's nationwide mandate or Estonia's comprehensive AI Leap program, the US relies on a patchwork of state and district initiatives with no federal coordination. This has resulted in massive disparities in access and quality.

Low Adoption Rates: Only 20% of American college students report using generative AI for their studies, compared to 63% in Kenya, 62% in Saudi Arabia and Spain, and 54% in Canada8. This adoption gap reflects both policy restrictions and cultural resistance.

Teacher Preparation Gap: A critical weakness is the lack of AI training in teacher education programs. As one report notes, "Not one superintendent we spoke with considered higher education a resource for artificial intelligence-related professional learning". This suggests a fundamental disconnect between higher education and K-12 needs.

Restrictive Policies: While other countries embrace AI as a learning tool, many US districts have implemented restrictive policies out of concerns about cheating, with some taking disciplinary action against students who use AI tool

The New Educational Arms Race

The stakes of educational disparity extend far beyond the classroom:

Economic Implications: AI-enabled education could boost GDP by approximately 6% in the long run according to research from the Tony Blair Institute. Countries that fail to equip their workforce with AI literacy risk significant economic disadvantages.

Workforce Vulnerability: By 2030, AI could automate 30% of US jobs in sectors like manufacturing and logistics.

Without proper AI training, American workers will be unprepared for this transition.

National Security Concerns: The comparison to the Space Race is China's AI education mandate which is what one expert calls "America's AI's competitive wakeup call". Unlike the Sputnik challenge, however, "America doesn't have years to catch up. AI advancements are happening at the fastest pace of any innovation in modern history".

Global Leadership at Risk: With China graduating twice as many STEM PhDs and countries like Estonia implementing nationwide AI literacy programs, America's technological leadership position is increasingly tenuous.

The Path Forward

For America to remain competitive in the new educational arms race, experts suggest several priority actions:

- **Federal Standards:** Implement national AI literacy standards similar to those adopted by other countries, while working within the US decentralized education system.
- **Teacher Training Revolution:** Invest heavily in AI professional development for educators at all levels, with special attention to teacher preparation programs.
- **Public-Private Partnerships:** Develop structured collaborations between tech companies and schools as seen in Estonia's AI Leap model.
- **Perspective Shift:** As Dr. Lisa Palmer of notes, America needs to "encourage this shift in the mindset around [AI] not being cheating, that this is how we're preparing our workforce for the future".

The global race to implement AI education represents what many experts are calling a new Sputnik moment for America - a challenge that will determine not just educational outcomes, but economic prosperity and national security for decades to come.

CHAPTER 22

WHERE WILL THE CLASS OF 2025 BE IN FIVE YEARS? CRAZY, SCARY, AND SPOOKY REALITIES

"We're not chasing our dreams anymore;
we're just trying to survive."
– Class of 2025 graduate

As of this writing, the class of 2025 is stepping into a job market unlike any before it—one shaped by technological disruption, economic uncertainty, and shifting societal priorities. As they graduate into a world where automation, AI, and global instability dominate headlines, these young professionals face both unprecedented challenges and emerging opportunities. The next five years will define not only their careers but also the broader trajectory of the global workforce.

Projected Job Distribution for the Class of 2025 by 2030

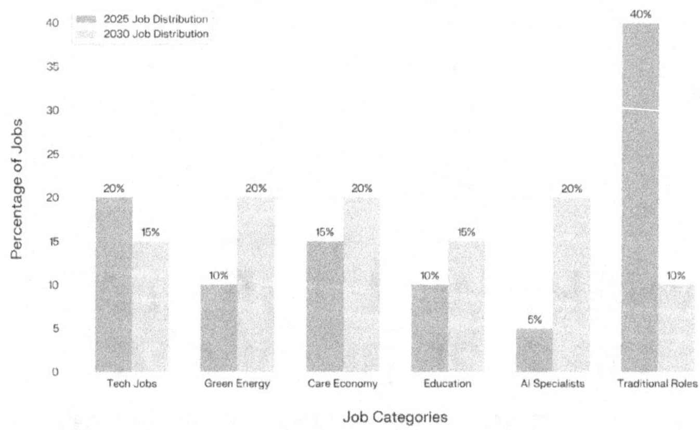

(Data Source: World Economic Forum)

The Current Landscape: A Shaky Start

Graduating into 2025's job market feels like stepping onto shifting sands. Economic uncertainty, driven by inflation, tariff wars, and automation, has reshaped industries across the board:

Tech Layoffs: Once the dream destination for many graduates, the tech industry has seen massive layoffs and hiring freezes. Applications for tech jobs have dropped significantly as Gen Z pivots toward other fields.

Government Instability: Elon Musk's Department of Government Efficiency (DOGE) has automated thousands of federal jobs, creating hiring freezes and intense competition for public sector roles.

Economic Ripple Effects: Nonprofits, universities, and businesses reliant on federal funding are scaling back hiring due to budget cuts and economic instability.

Psychological Toll: The uncertainty has left many graduates feeling hardened and anxious about their future, prioritizing job stability over passion.

The Five-Year Projection: Where Will The Class of 2025 Be in 2030?

By 2030, the Class of 2025 will have navigated a rapidly transforming labor market shaped by AI advancements, green energy initiatives, and human-centric roles in caregiving and education. The chart below illustrates how job distribution is expected to shift over the next five years:

Chart: Job Distribution Shift 2025 -2030

Projected Job Distribution	2025 Job Share	2030 Job Share
Tech Jobs	20%	15%
Green Energy	10%	20%
Care Economy	15%	20%
Education	10%	15%
AI Specialists	5%	20%
Traditional Roles	40%	10%

(Data Source: World Economic Forum)

Key Trends Driving Job Shifts:

1. **Decline in Traditional Roles:** Automation will replace many repetitive jobs in manufacturing, retail, and customer service (e.g., cashiers, data entry clerks).

2. **Rise of Green Energy:** Jobs in renewable energy (e.g., solar technicians, environmental engineers) will grow significantly as climate-change mitigation becomes a global priority.
3. **AI-Centric Careers:** Demand for AI specialists (e.g., machine learning engineers, big data analysts) will surge as companies integrate AI into every facet of their operations.
4. **Human-Centric Roles:** The care economy (nursing professionals, social workers) and education sectors will expand as aging populations and societal needs increase demand for human interaction and empathy-driven work.

Challenges Ahead for the Class of 2025

1. Increased Competition

Graduates will face stiff competition not only from their peers but also from experienced professionals displaced by automation or economic shifts. For example:

- Federal employees laid off by DOGE are now competing for entry-level government jobs.
- Tech workers transitioning out of traditional roles are flooding other industries.

2. Skills Gap

According to the The World Economic Forum's Future of Jobs Report 2025, by 2030, an estimated 44% of workers will need reskilling or upskilling to remain competitive. Employers are prioritizing skills like AI literacy, data analytics, cybersecurity, and creative problem-solving over traditional degrees.

3. Psychological Impact

The upheaval has already left many young people feeling disillusioned about their career prospects:

Opportunities on the Horizon

Despite these challenges, the next five years also present unique opportunities for those willing to adapt:

1. Skills-Based Hiring

Employers are increasingly valuing practical expertise over formal qualifications. This shift opens doors for graduates who invest in certifications or apprenticeships in high-demand areas like AI ethics or green technology.

2. Flexible Work Models

The WEF Future of Jobs Report also reveals that by 2030, an estimated 25% of global digital jobs will be fully remote. Flexible work arrangements will allow graduates to explore diverse career paths without being tied to specific locations.

3. Emerging Industries

Fields like green energy and AI are poised for explosive growth:

- Green energy roles (e.g., renewable energy engineers) are expected to double by 2030.
- AI-related jobs (e.g., machine learning specialists) will see some of the fastest growth rates across all sectors.

What Can Be Done? Solutions for Navigating This Reality

To ensure the success of the Class of 2025 over the next five years, action is needed at multiple levels:

For Students:

1. Embrace lifelong learning through online courses or bootcamps in emerging fields like AI or green energy.
2. Build adaptability by exploring hybrid roles that combine technical skills with creativity or empathy.

For Employers:

1. Invest in reskilling programs to prepare employees for new roles created by automation.
2. Develop latticed career paths that allow employees to move laterally across industries.

For Policymakers:

1. Expand funding for STEM education and green energy training programs.
2. Implement safety nets (e.g., universal basic income) to support workers displaced by automation.

Resilience Amidst Uncertainty

The Class of 2025 is entering a workforce defined by rapid change—a world where traditional roles are fading while new opportunities emerge in tech-driven and human-centric fields alike. By prioritizing adaptability and embracing lifelong learning, this generation has the potential to thrive amidst uncertainty.

As they navigate these "crazy, scary" realities over the next five years, one thing is clear: resilience will be their greatest asset in shaping not only their own futures but also the future of work itself.

CHAPTER 23

THE VALUE OF WORK IN 2025 AND ITS IMPACT ON MARGINALIZED DEMOGRAPHICS: BLACK, BROWN WORKERS, AND WOMEN

"We have to question not only who designs the tools but also who they are designed for and who they exclude."

– **Dr. Ruha Benjamin,** Professor of African American Studies, Princeton University

As work evolves in 2025, driven by advancements in artificial intelligence (AI), blockchain technology, and decentralized platforms, marginalized demographics such as Black workers, Brown workers, and women face unique challenges and opportunities. By 2030, these groups will experience significant shifts in their roles within the workforce due to automation, the gig economy, and new forms of decentralized collaboration.

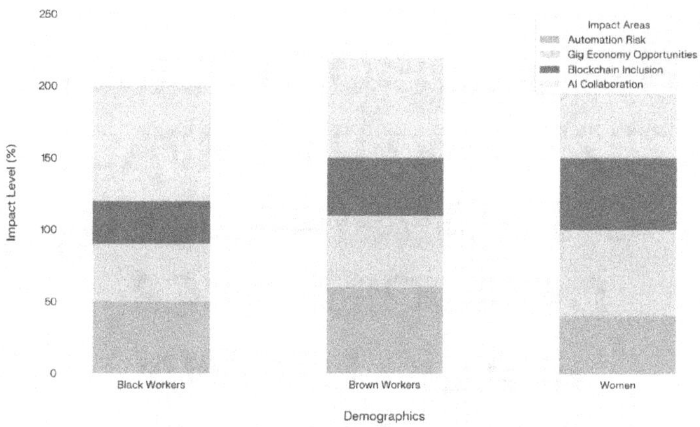

Impact of Work Value Changes on Demographics by 2030

The Current Landscape: Work in 2025

The value of work is being increasingly shaped by technological innovation and decentralization. Some of the key trends include:

- **Increased Automation**: Black and Brown workers are disproportionately represented in industries most vulnerable to automation, such as food services, office support roles, and production work. Without targeted reskilling programs, these groups risk significant job displacement.
- **Gig Economy Expansion**: The gig economy offers flexibility and global opportunities but lacks stability.

Women and minority workers often face lower earnings and fewer protections compared to their counterparts.

- **Blockchain Inclusion**: Blockchain technology provides access to decentralized financial systems for marginalized communities. Smart contracts enable secure transactions and equitable payment systems that can empower gig workers from underserved populations.
- **AI Collaboration:** AI integration is transforming workplaces. By 2030, working alongside intelligent systems will be as common as owning a smartphone today. However, without inclusive training programs, marginalized groups may struggle to access high-mobility AI-related roles.

The Impact: by 2030 and Beyond

1. Automation's Disproportionate Impact on Black and Brown Americans

Automation will displace millions of jobs traditionally held by Black and Brown workers:

- Nearly 4.5 million jobs that Black people in America currently hold could be displaced by 2030 due to overrepresentation in roles with high automation potential.
- Latino workers may see up to a quarter of their jobs automated out of existence in industries such as retail and customer service.

2. Blockchain Empowerment

Blockchain technology will enable financial inclusion for marginalized groups:

- Decentralized finance (DeFi) will provide access to global markets for gig workers while reducing reliance on intermediaries.

- Smart contracts can ensure fair compensation for women and minority workers while promoting transparency.

3. Gig Economy Challenges

The gig economy will intersect with decentralized platforms by 2030:

- Women will benefit from flexible work arrangements but may continue to face pay gaps unless structural barriers are addressed.
- Minority workers risk economic insecurity due to the lack of protections in gig work unless governments regulate these platforms effectively.

4. AI Collaboration

AI will become a collaborative partner rather than a replacement:

- Marginalized groups must navigate AI integration through upskilling initiatives to remain competitive.
- Organizations must focus on creating inclusive environments where humans and machines complement each other's strengths.
- Automation risks exacerbating inequalities unless reskilling initiatives prioritize Black and Brown workers.
- Blockchain-powered decentralized companies can democratize financial access for gig workers.
- Women can leverage decentralized platforms for leadership roles while addressing gender disparities.

Targeted policies that focus on reskilling marginalized demographics, promoting inclusivity in decentralized systems, and ensuring equitable access to emerging technologies are essential for fostering a future where all demographics thrive in the evolving workforce.

CHAPTER 24

PARTICIPATORY FUTURES: SHAPING THE FUTURE OF WORK

"The future is not something we enter. The future is something we create."
– **Alvin Toffler,** Futurist and Author

The future of work is not a predetermined path, but a landscape of possibilities shaped by the choices we make today. As we stand at the cusp of unprecedented technological advancements, particularly with the rise of artificial intelligence (AI), the need for participatory futures has never been more critical. This chapter explores how participatory futures can help us navigate the complexities of the evolving work landscape and ensure a more equitable and human-centered future.

What is 'Participatory Futures'?

Participatory futures is a framework that emphasizes the importance of involving diverse stakeholders—workers, employers, policymakers, educators, and communities—in envisioning and shaping the future of work. It's a collaborative approach that brings together a wide range of perspectives, values, and experiences to navigate the complexities of the evolving work landscape, especially in the context of rapid technological advancements like AI.

- **Key Idea**: Instead of passively accepting the future, we actively shape it.

Why Does Participatory Futures Matter?

Participatory futures is crucial because it provides a way to:

- **Anticipate and Mitigate AI's Negative Impacts**: Open dialogue and collaboration help identify potential risks (job displacement, algorithmic bias) and develop strategies for a just transition.
- **Harness AI's Positive Potential**: Participatory processes identify opportunities to leverage AI for social good (new jobs, improved working conditions, enhanced human capabilities).
- **Promote Equity and Inclusion**: Centering marginalized voices ensures that the benefits of technological progress are shared by all.
- **Foster Adaptability and Resilience**: Participatory processes help individuals and organizations develop the skills and mindsets needed to thrive in a rapidly changing world.
- **Strengthen Democratic Governance**: Participatory futures supports the development of more democratic and accountable institutions.

Benefits of a Participatory Future

A participatory approach offers numerous benefits, extending beyond mere economic considerations to encompass social, ethical, and personal dimensions:

- **Increased Legitimacy and Ownership**: When people are directly involved in shaping their future, they gain a sense of ownership over the outcomes. This leads to greater acceptance and support for policies and initiatives, fostering a more stable and cohesive society.

- **Improved Decision-Making**: By incorporating a wider range of perspectives, knowledge, and experiences, participatory processes lead to more robust, nuanced, and effective decisions. This reduces the risk of unintended consequences and ensures that policies are fit for purpose.
- **Enhanced Creativity and Innovation**: Bringing together people from diverse backgrounds sparks new ideas, challenges conventional thinking, and fosters innovation. This can lead to the development of novel solutions to complex problems, driving progress and growth.
- **Greater Social Cohesion**: Participatory processes build trust and understanding among different groups, bridging divides and fostering a sense of shared purpose and collective responsibility. This strengthens social bonds and promotes cooperation.
- **Empowered Individuals and Communities**: By giving people a voice in shaping their own futures, participatory futures promotes a sense of agency, autonomy, and empowerment. This enables individuals and communities to take control of their destinies and become active agents of change.
- **Ethical Considerations**: Participatory processes encourage a deeper consideration of the ethical implications of new technologies and policies. This helps to ensure that the future of work is shaped in a way that aligns with human values and promotes fairness and justice.
- **Long-Term Sustainability**: By considering the needs of current and future generations, participatory futures promotes sustainable development that bal-

ances economic growth with social and environmental well-being.

Participatory Future as a Solution for Displaced Workers

In the context of AI-driven job displacement, a participatory future offers a framework for proactive solutions, moving beyond reactive measures to address the root causes of displacement and empower affected workers:

1. **Risk Identification**: Identify jobs/skills vulnerable to automation through collaborative research and analysis, involving workers and industry experts. This goes beyond simply predicting job losses to understand the specific tasks and skills that are at risk.
2. **Solution Development**: Collaborate on solutions that go beyond traditional reskilling programs:
   - **Reskilling/Upskilling Programs**: Design programs in collaboration with workers, employers, and educational institutions, tailored to the specific needs of displaced workers and the demands of the future labor market. This includes not only technical skills but also soft skills like critical thinking, creativity, and adaptability.
   - **New Job Categories**: Foster the creation of new job categories and industries that leverage human skills in conjunction with AI, such as AI trainers, explainers, and ethicists. This requires a proactive approach to workforce development and innovation.
   - **Policies for Just Transition**: Develop policies that support displaced workers during the transition, such as:
     - **Universal Basic Income (UBI)**: Explore the potential of UBI in America that distributes the revenue gains made from AI, Automation and Robotics to the provide a safety net for workers

displaced– ensuring basic income to help offset the tens of millions of jobs eliminated by advancing technology.

- **Job Guarantee Programs**: Implement programs that guarantee employment for those who are displaced, providing them with meaningful work and a sense of purpose.
- **Portable Benefits**: Design benefits systems that are not tied to specific employers, allowing workers to move between jobs and adapt to changing labor market conditions.

- **Entrepreneurship Support**: Provide resources and support for displaced workers who wish to start their own businesses, fostering innovation and self-employment opportunities.

3. **Human-Centered AI**: Involve workers in the design and implementation of AI systems to ensure that technology complements and augments human capabilities, rather than simply replacing them. This includes:
   - **Worker Representation on AI Development Teams**: Include worker representatives on teams that design and develop AI systems to ensure that their perspectives and concerns are taken into account.
   - **Transparency and Explainability**: Advocate for AI systems that are transparent and explainable, allowing workers to understand how these systems work and how they affect their jobs.
   - **Ethical Guidelines**: Develop and implement ethical guidelines for the development and use of AI in the workplace, with input from workers and other stakeholders.

Benefits for BIPOC Individuals and Women

Participatory futures offers significant potential benefits for BIPOC (Black, Indigenous, and People of Color) individuals and women, who have historically been marginalized and underrepresented in the labor market and are often disproportionately affected by technological change:

- **Addressing Systemic Inequalities**: Participatory processes can help to identify and address the systemic inequalities that have historically disadvantaged BIPOC individuals and women in the workplace. This includes issues such as:
  - **Wage gaps**: Ensure that pay equity is a central consideration in the design of new jobs and policies.
  - **Occupational segregation**: Promote diversification in training and hiring to break down occupational segregation.
  - **Lack of access to training and education**: Provide targeted training and education programs to equip BIPOC individuals and women with the skills needed for the future of work.
  - **Bias in hiring and promotion**: Develop strategies to mitigate bias in AI-powered hiring and promotion systems.
- **Centering Marginalized Voices**: By centering the voices of BIPOC individuals and women, participatory futures can ensure that their specific needs and concerns are taken into account in the design of new technologies, policies, and programs. This can help to create a more equitable and inclusive future of work.
- **Empowerment and Agency**: Participatory processes can empower BIPOC individuals and women by giving them a greater sense of agency and control over their own economic futures. This can lead to increased economic security, social mobility, and overall well-being.
- **Building Community Wealth**: Participatory approaches can support the development of community-based economic development initiatives that bene-

fit BIPOC communities and women, fostering wealth creation and economic self-sufficiency.

Challenging Power Structures: Participatory futures can challenge existing power structures that perpetuate inequality, leading to a more just and equitable distribution of resources and opportunities.

New Approaches: The Five Pillars of Participatory Futures

To realize the benefits of participatory futures, we need new approaches that go beyond traditional methods. Here are five key pillars:

1. Play

- Emphasizes experimentation, creativity, and imagination.
- Uses playful methods (games, simulations, speculative design) to encourage unconventional thinking.
- **Examples**:
  - Future of Work Game Jams
  - Scenario planning workshops using role-playing
  - Design fiction projects

2. Immerse

- Creates immersive experiences to explore alternative futures.
- Uses technologies like VR/AR to create engaging encounters.
- **Examples**:
  - VR simulations of future workplaces
  - AR experiences overlaying future scenarios
  - Interactive exhibitions

3. Sense

- Focuses on gathering and interpreting diverse data about emerging trends.

- Employs techniques like ethnographic research, data visualization, and social media analysis.
- **Examples**:
  - Real-time labor market dashboards
  - Ethnographic studies of technology adaptation
  - Sentiment analysis of social media

4. Create

- Emphasizes building tangible artifacts that embody future visions.
- Uses prototyping, filmmaking, and storytelling to make future scenarios concrete.
- **Examples**:
  - Prototyping new tools/technologies
  - Documentaries about future workplaces
  - Interactive narratives

5. Deliberate

- Fosters dialogue, debate, and collective decision-making.
- Uses methods like citizens' juries, polls, and online forums.
- **Examples**:
  - Citizens' juries on future of work policies
  - Online platforms for stakeholder dialogue
  - Deliberative polls

Participatory Futures: A Path Forward

The future of work is at a critical juncture. The choices we make today will determine whether technological advancements lead to a more equitable and prosperous society or exacerbate existing inequalities and create new forms of hardship. Participatory futures offers a powerful framework for navigating this complex landscape and ensuring that the future of work is shaped in a way that benefits all members of society. By embracing the five pillars of play, immerse, sense, create, and deliberate, we can move beyond passively accepting the future and actively shape it in accordance with our values and aspirations. This is not merely a matter of economic efficiency; it is a matter of social justice, human dignity, and the creation of a world where everyone has the opportunity to thrive. Participatory futures matters because it provides a pathway to a future where work is not only productive and efficient but also equitable, sustainable, and fulfilling for all, especially for those who have been historically marginalized and underserved.

CHAPTER 25

BEYOND WORK

"All labor that uplifts humanity has dignity and importance and should be undertaken with painstaking excellence."
– Dr. Martin Luther King Jr.

Defining Work

Work, in its broadest sense, is purposeful activity—mental or physical—undertaken to achieve a goal, create value, or fulfill a responsibility. In science, work is the transfer of energy through force and movement. In society, it encompasses employment, caregiving, volunteering, and creative pursuits. Work is central to identity, meaning, and economic survival, but its role and definition have evolved dramatically over time.

Work in Sacred Texts

Work is a recurring theme in various sacred texts, each offering unique perspectives on its significance.

The Bible:

Work is depicted as a gift from God and a reflection of His creative activity. Genesis describes God as the first worker, creating the world in six days and resting on the seventh. Humans are tasked to "work and take care" of creation (Genesis 2:15). Work is inherently good, but after the Fall, it became toilsome—"by the sweat of your brow you will eat your food" (Genesis 3:19). Diligence is praised, and work is to be done for God's glory (1 Corinthians 10:31).

The Torah:

The Torah commands, "Six days you shall labor and do all your work" (Exodus 20:9). Work is both a duty and a blessing, with God promising prosperity through the work of one's hands (Deuteronomy 28:12, 30:9). The Sabbath principle balances work with rest, sanctifying both effort and renewal.

The Koran:

Islam regards work as a form of worship and a moral obligation. The Koran instructs believers to "work, for Allah will see your work" (Qur'an 9:105). Honest labor is highly valued, and reliance on others without effort is discouraged. Work is seen as a way to serve God and society, and earning a livelihood is considered virtuous.

How Work Has Changed Over the Past 100 Years

The last century has seen work transformed by industrialization, technology, and shifting social values.

Timeline of Work Evolution and Tasks Performed

Pre-Industrial Society (Pre-1760)

- Work centered on survival: hunting, gathering, farming, and household production.
- Labor was performed within families or small communities, often according to immediate needs.

- Tasks included growing food, making clothes, building shelter, and caring for children.

Industrial Revolution (1760–1840)

- Mechanization shifted work from home and farm to factories and urban centers.
- Tasks became repetitive and specialized: operating machines, assembling products, and factory maintenance.
- Workers often had little connection to the end product or ownership of their labor.

Rise of Offices and Bureaucracy (18th–20th Century)

- Emergence of dedicated office buildings for administration and paperwork (e.g., Old Admiralty Building in London).
- Tasks shifted toward clerical work, bookkeeping, and management.
- The division between manual labor and "white-collar" work became pronounced.

20th Century: Technological and Social Shifts

- Introduction of typewriters, telephones, and later computers changed the nature of office work.
- The mid-20th century saw structured 9-to-5 jobs, cubicles, and corporate hierarchies.
- The late 20th century brought automation, offshoring, and the rise of service and knowledge work.

Digital Age and Remote Work (1990s–2020s)

- Internet and mobile technology enabled remote work, gig economy, and flexible schedules.
- Tasks became more analytical, creative, and collaborative, with a shift toward problem-solving and communication.
- The pandemic accelerated hybrid and virtual work models, blurring boundaries between work and home.

Future of Work (2020s and Beyond)

- AI and automation continue to replace routine tasks, emphasizing uniquely human skills: creativity, empathy, adaptability.
- Workplaces are becoming more collaborative, digital, and centered on well-being and purpose.
- The concept of "work" is expanding to include multiple roles, lifelong learning, and portfolio careers.

What Happens Beyond Work?

Beyond work lies a reimagined life where identity, meaning, and fulfillment are not tethered solely to a job or employment. As technology automates more tasks and the boundaries between work and life blur, people are seeking:

- **Deeper Relationships**: Investing in family, friendships, and community.
- **Personal Growth:** Pursuing hobbies, learning, and creative passions.
- **Well-being:** Prioritizing mental, emotional, and physical health.
- **Service and Purpose:** Volunteering, mentoring, and contributing to causes beyond economic gain.
- **Spiritual Fulfillment:** Exploring faith, rest, and reflection as essential parts of a meaningful life.

This shift is a response to the stresses of digital overload, burnout, and the realization that work alone cannot sustain a meaningful existence. The future points toward a holistic integration of work and life, where professional roles are just one aspect of a rich, multifaceted human experience.

Are We Defined by Work? Insights from Sacred Scripture

Biblical Perspective

- The Bible teaches that work is a gift and a calling from God, but not the source of our ultimate identity.

Genesis shows Adam working in the garden before the fall, indicating that work is inherently good (Genesis 2:15).

- However, Scripture consistently warns against making work an idol. Colossians 3:23 urges believers to "work heartily, as for the Lord," but also reminds that our identity is in Christ, not in our occupations.
- Christians are called to be ambassadors for Christ in all areas of life, including work, but their value and purpose are rooted in being children of God, not in their job titles or achievements.

Torah and Koran

- The Torah upholds work as a duty and blessing, balanced with rest (Exodus 20:9-10). The Sabbath commandment sanctifies both labor and renewal, underscoring that humans are not defined solely by their productivity.
- The Koran views work as worship and moral responsibility but also emphasizes service to God and community, not personal status or wealth (Qur'an 9:105).

Sacred scripture affirms the dignity and importance of work but never equates a person's worth or identity with their occupation. Human value is anchored in relationship with God and others, not in what they produce or achieve.

Can Work Be Reshaped into Something Else?

Yes, work can—and is—being reshaped. The evolution of work shows a continual adaptation to new technologies, societal needs, and human aspirations. Today, work is being redefined to include:

- **Flexible and Hybrid Models:** Combining remote and in-person tasks.
- **Portfolio Careers:** Balancing multiple roles, side hustles, and creative projects.

- **Purpose-Driven Work:** Aligning tasks with personal values and societal impact.
- **Integration with Life:** Recognizing caregiving, volunteering, and learning as valuable forms of work.

This transformation is not just about efficiency or profit but about restoring balance, meaning, and dignity to human life.

#BeyondWork—A Biblical Vision

The Bible offers a vision where work is meaningful but not ultimate. Humans are called to steward creation, serve others, and reflect God's image through their labor. Yet, our deepest identity is found in communion with God and one another—not in our productivity or professional status.

As work continues to evolve, the challenge and opportunity is to shape lives where work serves as a means to love God, serve neighbors, and cultivate the gifts entrusted to us—not as the measure of our worth. Beyond Work lies rest, relationship, and the fullness of life that God intends.

"Work is a gift of God, not a punishment for sin. Even before the fall humanity [had] duties to perform. It was after God told Adam to be fruitful—by means of his work—that God declared that creation was 'very good' (Gen. 1:31)."

In conclusion, upskilling in robotics is essential for anyone seeking stability, advancement, and relevance in the rapidly evolving American job market-especially within BIPOC communities, who face both the greatest risks and the greatest opportunities as automation accelerates. Robotics is not just replacing traditional roles; it is creating entirely new career paths that did not exist a decade ago and will continue to do so at scale over the next five years.

Detailed Suggestions for Upskilling in Robotics:

- **Pursue Accessible Training:** Numerous high-quality robotics courses are available, ranging from free introductory programs to comprehensive, affordable certifications. Options include the Robotics Specialization by Penn (Coursera), project-based courses on Udemy, and advanced programs from MIT and Carnegie Mellon Robotics Academy, which also offer certifications recognized by industry leaders.

- **Apprenticeships and Hands-On Learning:** Programs like the ARM Institute's Robotics Technician Apprenticeship provide structured pathways to gain both classroom knowledge and practical, on-the-job experience, culminating in industry-recognized certifications.
- **Flexible Learning Formats:** Whether you prefer onsite, live online, or on-demand courses, institutions like Carnegie Mellon and Amazon's Upskilling 2025 initiative offer flexible options to fit different schedules and learning styles.
- **Community and Employer Support:** Seek out partnerships between local colleges, community organizations, and employers that offer targeted robotics training and mentorship for underrepresented groups, ensuring equitable access to these future-focused careers.

Pay and Benefits:

- **Competitive Salaries:** The average annual salary for a robotics technician in the U.S. is about $70,500, with entry-level positions starting around $51,800 and experienced professionals earning up to $96,000 or more. In states like California, salaries can be even higher, averaging $77,500.
- **Career Progression:** Robotics roles offer clear advancement paths. Increasing skills and experience can lead to higher pay, supervisory positions, and specialized roles in programming, maintenance, or system integration.

- **Job Security and Benefits:** Robotics jobs are in high demand and often come with strong benefits packages, including health insurance, retirement plans, and ongoing education support, as employers compete for skilled talent in a growing field.

Future Job Creation:

- Robotics and AI are projected to create nearly 97 million new jobs globally in the coming years, many of which do not yet exist today. These roles will span industries such as manufacturing, healthcare, logistics, and beyond, requiring a mix of technical, creative, and problem-solving skills.
- As automation takes over repetitive tasks, new jobs will emerge in system design, maintenance, AI optimization, and human-robot collaboration-fields that reward continuous learning and adaptability.

Why This Matters for BIPOC Communities:

- Proactive upskilling in robotics ensures BIPOC workers are not left behind by technological change but are instead positioned to lead and benefit from the next wave of job creation.
- Targeted training, mentorship, and equitable hiring practices can help close the opportunity gap and build generational wealth in communities historically underrepresented in STEM fields.

Bottom Line:

Robotics is not just about replacing jobs-it is about creating the careers of tomorrow. By investing in upskilling now, individuals and communities can secure higher-paying, future-proof roles and help shape an inclusive workforce for the next generation.

EPILOGUE

THE ALGORITHM IS REAL BY MIKE JOHNS

"Being like everybody is the same as being nobody."
– **Rod Serling,** Creator and producer
of *The Twilight Zone*

In a world where algorithms, AI, automation and robotics continue to advance at an unprecedented pace, the job market in 2030 will look drastically different from today. As highlighted in this book the rapid progression of AI and machine learning could render countless jobs obsolete, leaving millions of workers in search of new career paths.

I emphasize that entire industries may be disrupted or transformed, with robots and automation taking on tasks previously performed by humans. However, amidst the uncertainty, new opportunities and new approaches will arise for those who adapt and embrace the technological shift.

As we move towards a more data-driven society, it becomes crucial for professionals to develop new skills and knowledge in order to stay relevant. The rise of autonomous systems will undoubtedly redefine the roles and responsibilities of human workers, but it also presents a chance to rethink our definition and approach to work and create more fulfilling careers.

"Death of a Job," underscores the importance of fostering innovation, creativity, and continuous learning as we navigate the uncharted waters of the future. By doing so, we can not only survive but thrive in a world where artificial intelligence and other technology are reshaping the very nature of work.

While Ai, automation and robotics will undoubtedly replace certain routine tasks, it's also poised to create new, human-centric roles. In fact, some researchers predict that 70% of jobs in 2030 will be in fields that don't yet exist.

This shift is already evident in the rise of social media. Despite concerns about traditional media job losses, the social media industry now employs an estimated 21 million people worldwide. This trend underscores a crucial point: the challenge isn't a lack of human-only tasks, but rather the need for continuous adaptation and upskilling. Lifelong learning will be essential in this evolving landscape.

Automation is expected to drive down costs across various sectors, including finance, healthcare, mobility, food, and energy. This cost reduction, similar to what we've seen in media and content industries, could benefit consumers by reducing the need for increased paid work to maintain spending power.

Ideally, exponential technological progress could lead to a future with lower living costs and better-paid human-only tasks. However, realizing this potential will require wise governance and policy decisions.

On a personal level, it's important to embrace the coming changes with optimism.

Despite often negative portrayals in media, humans have historically shown remarkable adaptability when faced with new realities. The key is to acknowledge the ongoing changes and prepare accordingly.

To thrive in this new environment:

1. Embrace lifelong learning and continuous upskilling.

2. Stay agile and open to new career opportunities.
3. Focus on developing uniquely human skills that complement, rather than compete with, automation.
4. Understand that while some jobs may disappear, new ones will emerge.
5. Recognize that automation can lead to more fulfilling work by eliminating repetitive tasks.

By 2025, the World Economic Forum predicts that automation and AI could create at least 12 million more jobs than they eliminate. This aligns with historical patterns where technological advancements have ultimately led to job creation rather than widespread unemployment.

The Death of a Job is the Birth of a Future Reimagined

The "Death of a Job" is not merely about the disappearance of roles—it marks the transformation of work itself in the age of artificial intelligence. The White-Collar Recession of 2025 has demonstrated that AI is no longer just a tool but an autonomous workforce capable of reshaping industries at unprecedented speed. From finance and law to marketing and government, AI has displaced millions of traditional jobs while simultaneously creating new opportunities that demand advanced skills like critical thinking, creativity, and problem-solving.

This shift matters profoundly because it challenges the foundational structures of employment, education, and economic equity. While AI promises a net gain of 58 million jobs globally by 2025, it also risks widening the wealth gap and leaving behind those who lack access to upskilling opportunities. The transition requires intentional efforts to redefine how we prepare individuals for this new reality.

The Role of Communities in Reshaping Work

Local outreach organizations will play a pivotal role in addressing this disruption. Programs like Harlem's Uptown

Neighborhood Initiatives & Logistics, funded by the Center for Justice Innovation, exemplify how grassroots efforts can upskill communities and create pathways to emerging careers. Similarly, organizations such as the Urban League, Boys & Girls Clubs of America, Best Buy Teen Centers, community colleges, public libraries, and even informal Starbucks meet-ups are uniquely positioned to act as hubs for lifelong learning and workforce development. These institutions can:

- **Provide accessible training** in AI-related fields through workshops and certifications.
- **Foster collaboration** between local industries and educational programs to align curricula with market demands.
- **Bridge digital divides** by offering resources like broadband access and AI literacy programs to underserved populations.

A Call to Action

The death of traditional jobs does not have to mean the death of opportunity. Governments, corporations, and communities must work together to create systems that empower workers to adapt and thrive in our AI-driven economy. Policymakers should prioritize funding for upskilling initiatives and enforce transparency in AI deployment to mitigate bias and displacement risks. Employers must invest in retraining programs that prepare their workforce for collaboration with AI systems rather than replacement by them.

Ultimately, the future belongs to those who embrace change and commit to lifelong learning. By leveraging local networks and fostering innovation at every level—from grassroots organizations to global corporations—we can transform this period of disruption into one of empowerment. The "Death of a Job" is not an end but an opportunity to redefine work as we know it—creating a more inclusive economy where humans and machines coexist for mutual progress.

***

This book advocates for transformative investments to secure America's future by addressing systemic inequalities and equipping young people with the tools to thrive in an AI-driven world. It emphasizes the need to redesign education systems, integrating AI literacy into K-12 curricula across all 50 states, to provide students with critical skills for navigating a rapidly evolving workforce. The book also calls for targeted job creation for youth, particularly those not in education, employment, or training (NEETs), and strengthening institutions that support labor market transitions. By integrating employment initiatives with social protection systems and fostering nationwide cooperation through public-private partnerships and innovative financing models, it aims to tackle economic disparities and promote inclusive development. This comprehensive approach seeks to embed AI literacy into STEM education and professional development, enhancing learning, equity, and innovation across the country.

REFERENCES

Chapter 1 References

- *https://electroiq.com/stats/ai-replacing-jobs-statistics/*
- *https://www.whitehouse.gov/fact-sheets/2025/01/fact-sheet-president-donald-j-trump-takes-action-to-enhance-americas-ai-leadership/*
- *https://www.sandtech.com/insight/ai-and-the-future-of-work/*
- *https://www.bcg.com/publications/2019/artificial-intelligence-ai-help-hinder-women-workforce*
- *https://thefulcrum.us/media-technology/ai-jobs-training-trump*
- *https://www.govtech.com/artificial-intelligence/what-will-ai-policy-look-like-under-the-trump-administration*
- *https://www.aclufl.org/en/news/trumps-efforts-dismantle-ai-protections-explained*
- *https://www.mintz.com/insights-center/viewpoints/2226/2025-02-12-artificial-intelligence-executive-order-workplace*
- *https://thefulcrum.us/media-technology/ai-jobs-training-trump*
- *https://www.shrm.org/executive-network/insights/chro-response-trump-executive-order-diversity-ai-hiring-remote-work*

Chapter 2 References

- *https://www.brookings.edu/articles/one-year-later-how-has-the-white-house-ai-executive-order-delivered-on-its-promises/*
- *https://www.sidley.com/en/insights/newsupdates/2023/11/president-biden-signs-sweeping-artificial-intelligence-executive-order*
- *https://www.washingtoninformer.com/ai-responsible-development-biden-harris/*
- *https://www.squirepattonboggs.com/en/insights/publications/2025/02/key-insights-on-president-trumps-new-ai-executive-order-and-policy-regulatory-implications*
- *https://epic.org/google-rolls-back-responsible-ai-principles-breaking-promise-to-limit-military-use-of-its-products/*
- *https://www.washingtoninformer.com/ai-responsible-development-biden-harris/*
- *https://www.squirepattonboggs.com/en/insights/publications/2025/02/key-insights-on-president-trumps-new-ai-executive-order-and-policy-regulatory-implications*
- *https://www.whitehouse.gov/fact-sheets/2025/01/fact-sheet-president-donald-j-trump-takes-action-to-enhance-americas-ai-leadership/*
- *https://www.hunton.com/hunton-retail-law-resource/workplace-ai-presidential-change-and-unknown-expectations-for-retail-employers*

Chapter 3 References

- *https://www.route-fifty.com/artificial-intelligence/2025/01/generative-ai-government-what-expect-2025/402128/*
- *https://www.brookings.edu/articles/hollywood-writers-went-on-strike-to-protect-their-livelihoods-from-generative-ai-their-remarkable-victory-matters-for-all-workers/*

- *https://news.sky.com/story/almost-certain-civil-service-staff-numbers-will-be-cut-in-ai-efficiency-drive-minister-says-13327407*
- *https://www.forbes.com/sites/jasonwingard/2025/03/10/musk-replacing-workers-with-ai-should-you-be-worried/*

Chapter 5 References

- *https://linktr.ee/blog/linktree-creator-commerce-report*
- *https://www.benefitnews.com/news/how-tiktok-social-media-influencers-are-changing-the-workplace*
- *https://www.entrepreneur.com/business-news/what-is-gen-zs-no-1-career-choice-social-media-influencer/459387*
- *https://oot.live/2023/05/30/social-media-influencers-future-of-work/*
- *https://www.graydi.us/blog/graydata/trending-now-creator-economy-college-programs-are-growing*

Chapter 4 References

- *https://www.mckinsey.com/capabilities/mckinsey-digital/our-insights/superagency-in-the-workplace-empowering-people-to-unlock-ais-full-potential-at-work*

Chapter 6 References

- *https://www2.deloitte.com/content/dam/Deloitte/us/Documents/deloitte-analytics/us-consulting-women-in-ai.pdf*
- *https://www2.deloitte.com/us/en/insights/industry/technology/technology-media-and-telecom-predictions/2025/women-and-generative-ai.html*
- *https://www.womentech.net/how-to/what-could-rise-ai-mean-gender-equality-in-workplace-2025*
- *https://digitaldefynd.com/IQ/ai-role-in-women-empowerment/*
- *https://www.takeheleadwomen.com/blog/the-good-the-bad-and-the-promising-for-women-in-generative-ai-workforce*

Chapter 8 References

- *https://www.brookings.edu/articles/generative-ai-the-american-worker-and-the-future-of-work*
- *World Economic Forum's Future of Jobs Report 2025*
- *https://www.sandtech.com/insight/ai-and-the-future-of-work/*
- *https://explodingtopics.com/blog/ai-replacing-jobs*
- *https://www.aiprm.com/ai-replacing-jobs-statistics/*
- *https://seo.ai/blog/ai-replacing-jobs-statistics*
- *https://www.mckinsey.com/mgi/our-research/generative-ai-and-the-future-of-work-in-america*
- *https://venturebeat.com/ai/gradually-then-suddenly-is-ai-job-displacement-following-this-pattern/*
- *https://www.cbsnews.com/news/venture-capitalist-kai-fu-lee-ai-will-displace-40-percent-of-worlds-jobs-in-as-soon-as-15-years-60-minutes/*

Chapter 11 References

- *https://hai.stanford.edu/news/radical-proposal-universal-basic-income-offset-job-losses-due-automation*
- *https://www.peoplespolicyproject.org/2023/03/31/what-to-do-about-ai-driven-job-displacement/*
- *https://www.forbes.com/sites/cathyrubin/2024/07/17/can-universal-basic-income-save-us-from-the-destabilization-of-ai-and-automation/*

Chapter 12 References

- *https://digiday.com/media/gen-z-millennials-are-weak-link-as-ai-fuels-new-cyberattack-workplace-threats/*
- *https://pshra.org/survey-finds-gen-z-most-worried-about-ais-workplace-impact/*
- *https://www.forbes.com/sites/bryanrobinson/2025/02/19/gen-z-trust-ai-over-humans-in-their-careers-new-study-shows/*
- *https://writer.com/blog/generative-ai-survey-takeaways/*

- *https://insidehpc.com/2025/03/writer-survey-42-of-c-suite-say-gen-ai-is-tearing-their-companies-apart/*
- *https://writer.com/blog/enterprise-ai-adoption-survey/*
- *https://www.wftv.com/news/workplaces-adopt-ai-varying-rates-gen-z-is-ahead-curve/BWUNSX4FAJMWPNZAFOH3BBV5QM/*

Chapter 13 References

- *https://careerservices.cwu.edu/blog/2025/01/08/free-ai-courses/*
- *https://www.linkedin.com/pulse/best-free-paid-ai-certifications-courses-2025-anu-shreya-ztc1f*
- *https://www.linkedin.com/business/talent/blog/talent-acquisition/250-free-ai-courses*
- *https://www.techtarget.com/whatis/feature/10-top-artificial-intelligence-certifications-and-courses*

Chapter 14 References

- *https://www.consumeraffairs.com/movers/best-states-for-public-education.html*
- *https://www.impactlab.com/2025/01/23/ai-in-education-the-nigerian-pilot-program-that-could-transform-global-learning/*
- *http://opportunitynycha.org/events/free-vocational-training-adult-education-in-east-harlem/*
- *https://www.bgca.org/programs/education/*
- *https://raise.mit.edu/wp-content/uploads/2025/01/MIT_AIED_2024-Tianyi-Huang-Extracurricular-Success-of-Early-AI-Education.pdf*
- *https://hcz.org/our-programs/the-employment-and-technology-center/*
- *https://www.hcci.org/untitled-lmjmw*
- *https://www.umez.org/workforce-development*
- *https://blogs.nvidia.com/blog/ai-pathways-boys-girls-clubs-hudson-county/*

Chapter 15 References

- *https://www.ai4al.eu/artificial-intelligence-a-new-frontier-for-lifelong-learning/*
- *https://www.linkedin.com/pulse/fostering-lifelong-learning-adaptability-ai-driven-economy-thomas-vdsze*
- *https://news.darden.virginia.edu/2024/04/16/uva-darden-sands-institute-for-lifelong-learning-examines-ai-as-disruptive-force-in-talent-and-workforce-development/*
- *https://www.thedailystar.net/tech-startup/news/lifelong-learning-staying-relevant-the-age-ai-3821451*
- *https://www.unleash.ai/artificial-intelligence/from-superfans-to-rebels-meet-the-ai-user-personas-hr-leaders-need-to-know-about/*
- *https://www.salesforce.com/news/stories/ai-personas-at-work/*
- *https://thelettertwo.com/2024/09/05/the-five-types-of-ai-personas-youll-find-at-work/*
- *https://www.ai4al.eu/artificial-intelligence-a-new-frontier-for-lifelong-learning/*

Chapter 16 References

- *https://www.humanresourcesonline.net/most-in-demand-core-skills-globally-in-2025-2030*
- *https://www.muchskills.com/blog/skills-employers-looking-for-till-2025*
- *https://www.humanresourcesonline.net/most-in-demand-core-skills-globally-in-2025-2030*
- *https://www.weforum.org/publications/the-future-of-jobs-report-2025/in-full/3-skills-outlook/*
- *https://www.weforum.org/press/2025/01/future-of-jobs-report-2025-78-million-new-job-opportunities-by-2030-but-urgent-upskilling-needed-to-prepare-workforces/*
- *https://www.forbes.com/sites/rachelwells/2024/01/28/70-of-employers-say-creative-thinking-is-most-in-demand-skill-in-2024/*

- *https://www.art-xp.com/blog/discover-why-70-of-employers-say-creative-thinking-is-most-in-demand-skill-in-2024*
- *https://www.businessbecause.com/news/in-the-news/9647/essential-list-of-future-skills*
- *https://www.forbes.com/sites/rachelwells/2024/01/28/70-of-employers-say-creative-thinking-is-most-in-demand-skill-in-2024/*
- *https://www.weforum.org/press/2025/01/future-of-jobs-report-2025-78-million-new-job-opportunities-by-2030-but-urgent-upskilling-needed-to-prepare-workforces/*
- *https://www.muchskills.com/blog/skills-employers-looking-for-till-2025*
- *https://www.weforum.org/publications/the-future-of-jobs-report-2025/in-full/3-skills-outlook/*
- *https://www.weforum.org/publications/the-future-of-jobs-report-2025/in-full/3-skills-outlook/*
- *https://www.humanresourcesonline.net/most-in-demand-core-skills-globally-in-2025-2030*
- *https://www.businessbecause.com/news/in-the-news/9647/essential-list-of-future-skills*
- *https://www.weforum.org/press/2025/01/future-of-jobs-report-2025-78-million-new-job-opportunities-by-2030-but-urgent-upskilling-needed-to-prepare-workforces/*
- *https://www.humanresourcesonline.net/most-in-demand-core-skills-globally-in-2025-2030*
- *https://www.forbes.com/sites/rachelwells/2024/01/28/70-of-employers-say-creative-thinking-is-most-in-demand-skill-in-2024/*

Chapter 17 References

- *https://www.hypotenuse.ai/blog/what-jobs-will-ai-replace*
- *https://www.linkedin.com/pulse/top-jobs-most-risk-being-replaced-ai-kieran-gilmurray-9ashe*
- *https://www.resumeble.com/career-advice/jobs-that-will-be-gone-2030*

- *https://www.businessinsider.com/how-ai-could-affect-black-workers-job-replacement-fear-study-2023-11*
- *https://www.mckinsey.com/institute-for-economic-mobility/our-insights/the-impact-of-generative-ai-on-black-communities*
- *https://news.stthomas.edu/generative-ais-real-world-impact-on-job-markets/*
- *https://www.mckinsey.com/institute-for-economic-mobility/our-insights/the-impact-of-generative-ai-on-black-communities*
- *https://www.weforum.org/stories/2019/10/ai-automation-impact-african-american-workers/*
- *https://www.businessinsider.com/how-ai-could-affect-black-workers-job-replacement-fear-study-2023-11*

Chapter 19 References

- *https://www.nber.org/digest/dec05/great-inventions-come-later-life*

Chapter 20 References

- *https://e-estonia.com/estonia-announces-a-groundbreaking-national-initiative-ai-leap-programme-to-bring-ai-tools-to-all-schools/*
- *https://thenationaldesk.com/news/americas-news-now/american-college-students-lag-behind-in-ai-use-expert-calls-for-perspective-shift-in-education-chegg-anthology-survey-genai-chatgpt-openai-professors-kenya-canada-saudi-arabia-spain-united-kingdom-dr-lisa-palmer-mirko-widenhorn*
- *https://indianexpress.com/article/trending/top-10-listing/top-10-countries-leading-in-artificial-intelligence-ai-india-rank-9820641/*
- *https://www.the74million.org/article/new-research-finds-schools-of-education-fail-to-prepare-teachers-to-use-ai/*
- *https://institute.global/insights/economic-prosperity/the-economic-case-for-ai-enabled-education*

- *https://assets.ctfassets.net/75ila1cntaeh/1xp9M0JFLZfY-1WHleOW31u/3cb8763da221104a397a030096759411/Tony_Blair_Institute_for_Global_Change__The_Economic_Case_for_AI-Enabled_Education__July_2024.pdf*
- *manufacturing and logistics9. Without proper AI training, American workers will be unprepared for this transition.*
- *https://www.the74million.org/article/ai-education-is-the-new-space-race-heres-how-america-must-respond/*
- *https://e-estonia.com/estonia-announces-a-groundbreaking-national-initiative-ai-leap-programme-to-bring-ai-tools-to-all-schools/*

Chapter 22 References

- *https://www.weforum.org/publications/the-future-of-jobs-report-2025/in-full/2-jobs-outlook*

Chapter 23 References

- *https://www.weforum.org/stories/2019/10/ai-automation-impact-african-american-workers/*
- *https://www.cbsnews.com/news/automation-why-automation-could-hit-black-workers-harder-than-other-groups/*
- *https://www.culturebanx.com/cbx-daily/workforce-automation-is-exacerbating-the-racial-wealth-gap/*
- *https://londonpolitica.com/esg-watch-blog-list/blockchain-social-mobility*
- *https://londonpolitica.com/esg-watch-blog-list/blockchain-social-mobility*
- *https://sustainability-directory.com/term/blockchain-for-inclusion/*
- *https://www.b2econsulting.com/what-is-the-impact-of-the-gig-economy-on-women-who-work-in-it-and-will-it-help-narrow-the-gender-gap/*
- *https://www.nature.com/articles/s41598-022-12558-x*
- *http://cdn-odi-production.s3.amazonaws.com/media/documents/12586.pdf*

- *https://info.jff.org/hubfs/JFF-AI-Ready%20Workforce%20Report_103123-vF.pdf*
- *https://pmc.ncbi.nlm.nih.gov/articles/PMC11852158/*

Chapter 25 References

- *https://www.alamy.com/stock-photo/pre-industrial.html*
- *https://www.archives.gov/exhibits/way-we-worked/*
- *https://www.focusonthefamily.com/parenting/what-does-it-mean-to-have-a-biblical-view-of-work/*
- *https://digital-skills-jobs.europa.eu/en/community/online-discussions/robots-taking-jobs-creating-careers*
- *https://edisonandblack.com/pages/over-97-million-jobs-set-to-be-created-by-ai.html*
- *https://builtin.com/artificial-intelligence/ai-replacing-jobs-creating-jobs*
- *https://standardbots.com/blog/robotics-training*
- *https://www.cmu.edu/roboticsacademy/news/cmra-news-2024/2025_training_schedule.html*
- *https://arminstitute.org/projects/robotics-technician-apprenticeship-program/*
- *https://digital-skills-jobs.europa.eu/en/community/online-discussions/robots-taking-jobs-creating-careers*
- *https://www.aboutamazon.com/news/workplace/our-upskilling-2025-programsthese future-focused careers*
- *https://www.salary.com/research/salary/posting/robotics-technician-salary*
- *https://www.payscale.com/research/US/Job=Robotics_Technician/Hourly_Rate*
- *https://www.salary.com/research/salary/posting/robotics-technician-salary/ca*
- *https://builtin.com/artificial-intelligence/ai-replacing-jobs-creating-jobs*

Epilogue References

- *https://edisonandblack.com/pages/over-97-million-jobs-set-to-be-created-by-ai.html*
- *https://www.linkedin.com/pulse/automation-catalyst-job-creation-across-five-industries-jeff-bell-ps6ne*
- *https://www.weforum.org/stories/2022/09/how-automation-job-creation-hand-in-hand/*
- *https://www.bulbtech.com/2023/04/17/impact-of-automation-will-it-create-more-jobs-than-it-destroys/*
- *https://builtin.com/artificial-intelligence/ai-replacing-jobs-creating-jobs*
- *https://fee.org/articles/automation-replaced-800-000-workers-then-it-created-35-million-new-jobs/*
- *https://www.forbes.com/councils/forbesbusinesscouncil/2023/07/26/how-does-artificial-intelligence-create-new-jobs/*

ACKNOWLEDGMENTS

I've had the privilege of learning from extraordinary individuals who have shaped my perspective and fueled my passion for writing this book. Texas Representative Giovanni Capriglione taught me the importance of leadership and integrity in public service. Salim Ismail, the exponential strategist, opened my mind to the transformative power of disruptive technologies. Dr. Sylvester James Gates, a theoretical physicist, revealed the beauty of understanding the universe through science and mathematics. Sophia the Robot reminded me of the boundless possibilities of human creativity and artificial intelligence. Retired Brigadier General Arnold Bray exemplified resilience and leadership in the face of adversity. I acknowledge Inventor Coach and Mastermind, Lisa Lloyd; Professor Frans von der Dunk, who has inspired me with his vision for *Space Law* and its role in humanity's future beyond Earth; and Dr. Ben Goertzel, who has demonstrated how AI can be democratized for the betterment of society.

Each of these remarkable figures has left an indelible mark on me, but none more profoundly than my son. You are my North Star, the reason I strive to leave a legacy that educates, inspires, and uplifts others.

I am very grateful to my editor, Anita S. Lane, for helping to bring this project to fruition. Special thanks to my colleague, Noleen Mariappen, for generously dedicating her time to reviewing the manuscript. And to my mother—my first love—thank you for always looking out for your son, and for still catching my typos after all these years. From Jamaica to the world, to the future – *One Luv*!

This book is a labor of love—a testament to the lessons I've learned in the field, from the brilliant minds in my life and our shared journey to explore what's possible. It is my hope that this work not only educates and inspires others but also serves as a lasting contribution to the culture—a legacy that encourages curiosity, innovation, and growth for generations to come.

AUTHOR BIO

Mike Johns is a futurist, educator, and cultural strategist committed to helping people—and the communities they live in—thrive in the age of AI. As founder of the creative agency Digital Mind State, Mike has spent two decades at the intersection of innovation, media, and culture, working with brands like Shell, Samsung, T-Mobile, Microsoft and iHeart Radio to elevate their voices and connect meaningfully with next-gen consumers.

He's the executive producer of the *"Yo! Tech This Out!"* Podcast, and *Tech With Soul* – platforms that connect emerging technology, startups and culture. Through these initiatives, Mike advocates for a future where technology meets culture and equity stands strong, and where people of all colors are not left behind by automation, but positioned at the forefront of it.

Mike wrote *Death of a Job* as both a wake-up call and a survival guide to help everyday people navigate the collapse of traditional employment and reimagine work on their own terms. His aim is to inspire reinvention, not fear.

He also serves as a professor and public speaker, known for his candid, street-smart insights on AI, digital disruption, and what it means to find purpose in a post-job world.

- Connect with Mike Johns and the #BeyondWork community at *www.DeathofAJob.com*
- Connect with Mike on LinkedIn at *linkedin.com/in/mikejohns*
- Learn more about Mike Johns at *www.MikeJohns.ceo*

#DeathofAJob #BeyondWork

CAIPA

Consumer AI Protection Advocates

ConsumerAIProtection.org

On December 9, 2024, Mike Johns posted a **now-viral video on LinkedIn** capturing his harrowing experience inside a **malfunctioning autonomous Waymo vehicle** that began driving in circles.

Mike's video ultimately achieved nearly 1 Billion views worldwide. It also resulted in a private meeting with top Waymo executives.

While Mike's story gained visibility and sparked dialogue, he quickly recognized that many others impacted by AI, autonomous vehicles, and robotics often go unheard. Their stories—equally unsettling—rarely garner attention, let alone accountability.

Thus, motivated by a commitment to transparency, equity, and ethical oversight, Mike launched **Consumer AI Protection Advocates (CAIPA)** in early 2025. CAIPA's mission is to empower consumers by advocating for responsible AI practices that safeguard consumer rights and interests across various sectors, including electric vehicles (EVs), autonomous vehicles (AVs), and robotics.

CAIPA exists to address a broad range of AI-related issues affecting consumers in EVs, AVs, and robotics, including data privacy, algorithmic bias, and emerging risks. CAIPA operates independently, working across these sectors to ensure that consumer voices are heard and valued in AI policy discussions.

To learn more and to get involved visit:
www.ConsumerAIProtection.org.

www.ingramcontent.com/pod-product-compliance
Lightning Source LLC
LaVergne TN
LVHW011512200926
848484LV00001B/18